The Classical Influence in English Literature in the Nineteenth Century
and Other Essays and Notes

By

WILLIAM CHISLETT, Jr., Ph.D.

1918

THE STRATFORD COMPANY

BOSTON

Copyright 1918
The STRATFORD CO., Publishers
Boston, Mass.

The Alpine Press, Boston, Mass., U. S. A.

Foreword

THE author hopes that in spite of overcrowding in some of them, and slightness of treatment in others, these essays and notes, certain of which have already appeared separately, may be of interest in collected form.

CONTENTS
PART I.

The Classical Influence in English Literature in the Nineteenth Century

	Page
I. INTRODUCTION	1
1. Classicism, Romanticism and Realism	1
2. Classicism, Romanticism and Realism in Greek and Latin Literature	2
3. Classicism, Romanticism and Realism in the Middle Ages, the Renaissance and Modern Times	3
4. Classicism, Romanticism and Realism in English Literature	5
II. THE ROMANTICISTS	
1. Samuel Taylor Coleridge (1772-1834)	8
2. William Wordsworth (1770-1850)	8
3. William Godwin (1756-1836)	8
4. Percy Bysshe Shelley (1792-1822)	9
5. Thomas Love Peacock (1785-1866)	9
6. John Keats (1795-1821)	9
7. George Gordon, Lord Byron (1788-1824)	9
8. Robert Southey (1774-1843)	10
III. MAJOR PROSE WRITERS, EXCLUSIVE OF THE NOVELISTS	
1. Charles Lamb (1775-1834)	11
2. William Hazlitt (1778-1830)	11

CONTENTS

	Page
3. Thomas De Quincy (1785-1859)	11
4. Walter Savage Landor (1775-1864)	11
5. Thomas Babington Macaulay (1800-1859)	12
6. Thomas Carlyle (1795-1881)	12
7. John Henry Newman (1801-1890)	12
8. Matthew Arnold (1822-1888)	12
9. John Ruskin (1819-1900)	13
10. Walter Pater (1839-1894)	13
11. Oscar Wilde (1856-1900)	13

IV. MAJOR VICTORIAN POETS

1. Alfred, Lord Tennyson (1809-1892)	15
2. Elizabeth Barrett Browning (1806-?-1861)	15
3. Robert Browning (1812-1889)	16
[4. Dante Gabriel and Christina Rossetti (1828-1882; 1830-1894)]	16
5. William Morris (1834-1896)	16
6. Algernon Charles Swinburne (1837-1909)	17

V. THE NOVELISTS

1. Maria Edgeworth (1767-1849)	18
2. Sir Walter Scott (1771-1832)	18
3. Jane Austen (1775-1817)	18
4. Charlotte and Emily Brontë (1816-1855; 1818-1848)	18
5. Mary Russell Mitford (1787-1855)	18
6. Elizabeth Cleghorn Gaskell (1810-1865)	18
7. William Makepeace Thackeray (1811-1863)	18
8. Charles Dickens (1812-1870)	19
9. George Eliot (1819-1880)	19
10. Edward Bulwer, Lord Lytton (1803-1873)	20
11. Edward Robert Bulwer Lytton: "Owen Meredith" (1831-1891)	20

CONTENTS

	Page
12. Benjamin Disraeli, Earl of Beaconsfield (1804-1881)	20
13. Anthony Trollope (1815-1882)	20
14. Charles Kingsley (1819-1875)	21
15. Charles Reade (1814-1884)	21
16. Wilkie Collins (1824-1889)	21
17. Robert Louis Stevenson (1850-1894)	21
18. Eliza Lynn Linton (1822-1898)	21
19. Richard Doddridge Blackmore (1825-1900)	21
20. Sir Walter Besant (1836-1901)	21
21. George Gissing (1857-1903)	22
22. William Sharp: "Fiona Macleod" (1855-1905)	22
23. George Meredith (1828-1909)	22
24. Thomas Hardy (1840-)	22
25. Mrs. Humphrey Ward (1851-)	22
26. George Moore (1853-)	23
27. Rudyard Kipling (1865-)	23
28. H. G. Wells (1866-)	23
29. Maurice Hewlett (1861-); Eden Phillpotts (1862-); Sir Arthur Quiller-Couch (1863-); Note on Lesser Novelists (*Cambridge History of English Literature*, vols. XII-XIII)	23

VI. MINOR WRITERS

1. Henry Kirke White (1875-1806)	24
2. Felicia Dorothea Hemans (1793-1835)	24
3. Winthrop Mackworth Praed (1802-1839)	24
4. Thomas Campbell (1777-1844)	24
5. Thomas Hood (1799-1845)	24
6. Sydney Smith (1771-1845)	24

CONTENTS

	Page
7. Isaac D'Israeli (1766-1848)	24
8. Hartley Coleridge (1796-1849)	24
9. Thomas Lovell Beddoes (1803-1849)	24
10. Francis Jeffrey (1773-1850)	24
11. Thomas Moore (1779-1852)	25
12. James Montgomery (1771-1854)	25
13. John Wilson: "Christopher North" (1785-1854)	25
14. Samuel Rogers (1763-1855)	25
15. Leigh Hunt (1784-1859)	25
16. Arthur Hugh Clough (1819-1861)	25
17. Bryan Waller Proctor: "Barry Cornwall" (1787-1874)	25
18. Sydney Dobell (1824-1874)	25
19. Robert Stephen Hawker (1803-1875)	26
20. Walter Bagehot (1826-1877)	26
21. George Borrow (1803-1881)	26
22. Arthur O'Shaughnessy (1844-1881)	26
23. James Thomson (1834-1882)	26
24. Edward FitzGerald (1809-1883)	26
25. Charles Stuart Calverley (1831-1884)	26
26. Richard Monckton Milnes, Baron Houghton (1809-1885)	26
27. Richard Jefferies (1848-1887)	27
28. Eliza Cook (1818-1889)	27
29. William Allingham (1824-1889)	27
30. John Addington Symonds (1840-1893)	27
31. Frederick Locker-Lampson (1821-1895)	27
32. John Byrne Leicester Warren, Lord De Tabley (1835-1895)	27
33. Coventry Patmore (1823-1896)	28
34. Thomas Edward Brown (1830-1897)	28
35. Frederick Tennyson (1807-1898)	28

CONTENTS

		Page
36. Grant Allen (1848-1899)	. . .	28
37. H. D. Trail (1842-1900)	. . .	28
38. Robert Williams Buchanan (1841-1901)	.	28
39. Aubrey de Vere (1814-1902)	. . .	28
40. Philip James Bailey (1816-1902)	. .	28
41. Samuel Butler (1835-1902)	. . .	28
42. William Ernest Henley (1849-1903)	. .	29
43. Ernest Dowson (1867-1900)	. . .	29
44. Lionel Johnson (1867-1902)	. . .	29
45. Sir Edwin Arnold (1832-1904)	. .	29
46. Lafcadio Hearn (1850-1904)	. . .	29
47. Sir Lewis Morris (1833-1907)	. .	29
48. Francis Thompson (1859-1907)	. .	30
49. John Davidson (1857-1909)	. . .	30
50. Andrew Lang (1844-1912)	. . .	30
51. Edward Dowden (1843-1913)	. . .	30
52. Alfred Austin (1835-1913)	. . .	30
53. George Otto Trevelyan (1838-) .	.	30
54. John Todhunter (1839-)	. . .	30
55. Austin Dobson (1840-)	. . .	30
56. Robert Bridges (1844-)	. . .	31
57. W. H. Mallock (1849-)	. . .	31
58. Edmund Gosse (1849-)	. . .	31
59. F. B. Money-Coutts (1852-)	. .	31
60 George Bernard Shaw (1856-)	. .	31
61. William Watson (1858-)	. . .	31
62. George William Russell: "A.E." (1867-)	31
63. Kenneth Grahame (1859-)	. .	31
64. Arthur Symons (1865-)	. . .	31
65. Arthur Waugh (1866-)	. . .	32
66. Hubert Crackanthorpe (1870-1896)	. .	32
67. Richard Le Gallienne (1866-)	. .	32
68. William Butler Yeats (1866-)	. .	32

CONTENTS

	Page
69. Stephen Phillips (1868-1915)	32
70. Lawrence Binyon (1869-)	32
71. George Macaulay Trevelyan (1876-)	32
72. Additional poets from Arthur Symons' *The Romantic Movement in English Poetry*	
(1) William Gifford (1756-1826)	32
(2) John Hookham Frere (1769-1846)	32
(3) James Hogg (1770-1835)	32
(4) Mrs. Tighe (1772-1810)	32
(5) Henry Francis Cary (1772-1844)	32
(6) John Leyden (1775-1811)	33
(7) Horace Smith (1779-1849)	33
(8) Robert Eyres Landor (1781-1869)	33
(9) Edward, Baron Thurlow (1781-1829)	33
(10) James Sheridan Knowles (1784-1862)	33
(11) Henry Hart Milman (1791-1868)	33
(12) William Maginn (1793-1842)	33
(13) Thomas Noon Talfourd (1795-1854)	33
(14) John Hamilton Reynolds (1796-1852)	33
73. Additional Poets from Miles' *The Poets and Poetry of the Century*	
(1) Edwin Atherstone (1788-1872)	33
(2) Richard Henry Horne (1803-1884)	33
(3) Richard Chevenix Trench (1807-1886)	33
(4) Charles Tennyson Turner (1808-1879)	33
(5) John Stuart Blackie (1809-1895)	33
(6) Thomas Gordon Hake (1809-1895)	33

CONTENTS

	Page
(7) Sir Francis Hastings Doyle (1810-1888)	33
(8) Alfred Domett (1811-1887)	34
(9) Arthur Henry Hallam (1811-1833)	34
(10) William James Linton (1812-1897)	34
(11) Thomas Westwood (1814-1888)	34
(12) Sir Joseph Noel Paton (1821-1901)	34
(13) Dora Greenwell (1821-1882)	34
(14) Thomas Woolner (1825-1892)	34
(15) Mortimer Collins (1827-1876)	34
(16) Richard Watson Dixon (1833-1900)	34
(17) John Nichol (1833-1894)	34
(18) Richard Garnett (1835-1906)	34
(19) Thomas Ashe (1836-1889)	34
(20) David Gray (1838-1861)	34
(21) Herman Charles Merivale (1839-1906)	34
(22) A. Mary F. Robinson-Darmesteter (1857-)	34
(23) Mrs. Ernest Radford (1858-)	34
(24) "Michael Field" (-)	34
(25) Alice Meynell (1850-)	34
74. Additional Poets from F. St. John Corbett's *A History of English Poetry*, 1904.	
(1) William Sotheby 1757-1833)	34
(2) Thomas Mitchell (1783-1845)	35
(3) John Edmund Reade (1800-1870)	35
(4) Rev. Henry Alford (1810-1871)	35
(5) Rev. George Croly (1780-1860)	35
75. Note on Additional Material from vols. XII and XIII of *The Cambridge History of English Literature*	35

CONTENTS

VII. CONCLUSION
    1. Classicism in the Romantic-realistic Nineteenth Century 36
    2. The Spirit of Greece 39
    3. The Spirit of Rome 44
    4. The Permanence of the Classical Tradition 47

CONTENTS

PART II.

Other Essays and Notes

	Page
I. The Platonic Love of Walter Pater	51
II. The New Hellenism of Oscar Wilde	60
III. The New Christianity of William Blake	69
IV. The Influence of William Blake on William Butler Yeats	88
V. William Vaughn Moody's Feeling for the Seventeenth Century	96
VI. William Vaughn Moody and William Blake	107
VII. On Moody's Men and Women	110
VIII. The Work of Robert Bridges	115
IX. Alas, Poor Yorick!	123
X. In Praise of Euphranor	128
XI. Walter Savage Landor, Eliza Lynn Linton and Julia Landor	131
XII. The Influence of Nonnus on Elizabeth Barrett Browning, Thomas Love Peacock and Walter Pater	136
XIII. A Minor Note in Arthur Symons	140
XIV. The Major Note in Thomas Hardy	142

PART I

The Classical Influence in English Literature in the Nineteenth Century

I

Introduction

1. *Classicism, Romanticism and Realism.*

NOTHING is less final than the classification of an author as a classicist, a romanticist or a realist; for every writer, ancient, mediaeval, Renaissance or modern, has classical, romantic and realistic strains in his life and works. The classical Horace had romantic[1] and realistic elements;[2] the realist Zola had classical[3] and romantic[4] qualities. Yet Horace is predominantly classical, and Zola is preëminently realistic.

To define classicism, romanticism and realism in general is as difficult as to apply the terms in any comprehensive sense when defined. If we say, for example, that classicism is the embodiment of Greece and Rome in later literatures, we state a half-truth; for much of the influence of Greece and Rome is romantic and realistic. Plato's effect on later ages, for instance, and Euripides', have been chiefly romantic, Juvenal's realistic.

Nevertheless, for the purposes of a study like the present, we should attempt definitions of the three terms,—albeit with classical brevity.

Classicism, then, means limitation of subject, adherence to established form, order, reason, restraint, simplicity, clarity, soberness and good sense. The literatures of

---

[1] e. g., His love for his Sabine farm.
[2] His description of Priapus and the witches, "Satires," Bk. I, viii; etc., etc. (See Voltaire's "Candide," Pt. I, Ch. XXV.)
[3] His style often has classical clarity.
[4] A tendency to sensationalism.

Introduction

Greece, Rome, and France are predominantly, but by no means solely, classical.

Romanticism involves impatience with limitation, rule, order, reason, soberness, and restraint and shows a preference for strangeness, emotion, imagination, fancy, intuition, mysticism, individualism, passion, and sentimentalism, Nature, humanitarianism, impulse, revolution, liberty and even license. The literatures of England and Germany are more innately romantic than classical.

Realism supports the evidence of the senses and records facts that have been observed and verified. It marks the supplanting of classical authority and romantic imagination by Science. To the realist the individual is neither constrained by precept nor freed by positing his own world, but is the product of his inheritance and environment. Realism and naturalism flourished in France, Russia, Germany and to a lesser degree in England, during the second half of the nineteenth century. In the nineties, however, it was opposed by Symbolism, or Modern Romanticism, with its theories of impressionism and mysticism. The current free-verse movement, though romantic in form, is often realistic in subject and content.

2. *Classicism, Romanticism and Realism in Greek and Latin Literature.*

Greek Literature, and Roman Literature, its close follower in this respect, was a literature of types. Tradition set the type for epic, for lyric, for philosophy, for oratory, for bucolic poetry. "You that write," says Horace in his *Art of Poetry*, "either follow tradition or invent such things as are congruous in themselves."[5] . . . Turn over the

[5] l. 119.

Introduction

Greek models by night, turn them by day."[6] Later he adds, "To have good sense is the first principle and fountain of writing well."[7]

With the type fixed,[8] and good sense as their acknowledged or unexpressed principle of writing, the ancients usually observed the other rules which we call classical. Proportion, reason, clarity, soberness and restraint characterize their work. Yet to say that the Greeks and Romans were always reasonable, always sober, always restrained is to misrepresent them. The philosophers and historians were not always reasonable, the dramatists and Pindar and the Latin language were not always simple, Euripides was not always sober, nor Cicero restrained.

Romanticism, in fact, is present in all its forms in Greek and Latin. There is fancy in Homer, imagination in Lucretius, melancholy, emotion, sentiment and sentimentality in Euripides; love of liberty in Socrates and Demosthenes and feeling as well as thought in Virgil.

And who will deny that there is realism in Homer, Virgil, Plato, Aristotle, the tragedians, the comedians, the historians, philosophers, lyric poets, bucolic poets and anthologists? Not the developed realism, to be sure, of modern science, but the realism, at least, of certain facts observed and carefully recorded. As for Petronius and Alciphron, they are almost modern in their realism.

3. *Classicism, Romanticism and Realism in the Middle Ages, the Renaissance and Modern Times.*

In the Middle Ages the classical spirit was ascertained not essentially through Sophocles, Plato and Horace, but

---
[6] ll. 268-9.   [7] l. 309.
[8] R. K. Hack: "The Doctrine of Literary Forms," ("Harvard Studies in Classical Philology," vol. XXVII, pp. 1-65,) holds that undue emphasis has been placed on Types.

Introduction

through Aristotle, Virgil, Ovid, the younger Pliny, Boethius, the Tale of Troy and the Legend of Alexander. In the cloister schools the Greek alphabet was occasionally learned; in Ireland and Southern Italy Greek authors were read; while the study of Latin literature among scholars, and in monasteries generally, was fairly extensive; including, for example, Terence, Cicero, Livy, Horace, Juvenal and Persius. Bede, Scotus Erigena, Gerbert, Rabanus Maurus, John of Salisbury and Roger Bacon were good classical scholars. Something of Plato was known, through a Latin version of part of the *Timaeus*. But the predominant note of the period was romantic. Even the Classics appealed romantically. Ovid was a story-teller, Virgil a magician and sage, Lucan and Statius were supreme epic poets. Yet the distinctive literary form was none of these, but the extravagantly romantic epic of chivalry. Meantime the seeds of modern realism were sown. With the rise of the towns realistic *fabliaux*, farces, mysteries, and moralities appeared.

At the Renaissance the classical revival, already well under way in Italy through Petrarch, Boccaccio and visiting scholars from Byzantium, burst forth in splendor; yet the Amadis of Gaul continued the romantic movement and Rabelais the realistic.

In the classical seventeenth and eighteenth centuries Aristotle, Horace, and Quintilian served as teachers of rule, order and propriety. In the nineteenth an almost Renaissance revival of scholarship occurred, but one tempered with a finer critical sense; with a surer understanding of ancient life and literature; with a concern with spirit as much as letter. Meantime the end of the eighteenth century and much of the nineteenth witnessed the beginnings and the triumph of romanticism,—the freedom of the individual and a corresponding freedom in art. Democracy,

Introduction

moreover, continued to be reflected in part during the classical centuries, until, in the nineteenth, realism, especially in France, grew till it flowered in Balzac, Zola, Tolstoy, Hardy, and many others,—in George Moore and Hubert Crackanthorpe, among them.

4. *Classicism, Romanticism and Realism in English Literature.*

In its literary and religious movements England has been ahead of and behind the continent in point of time. Both Renaissance and Reformation were anticipated in a general way by Chaucer and Wycliffe; yet the Revival of Learning, and the Renaissance proper in the Age of Elizabeth followed the Italian Renaissance at some distance. Again, while the age of classicism in France was essentially the seventeenth, in England it was the eighteenth. These differences from the continent gave England opportunity for that independent development that makes her literature peculiarly original, personal and individualistic.

Early English Christian poetry was largely dependent on the Vulgate and mediaeval Latin sources. Beowulf was by turns romantic and realistic, and metrical romances were chiefly romantic. In general, Chaucer was the romanticist, Gower the classicist, Langland the realist of their age. Visions and lyrics were romantic; *fabliaux,* mysteries, and moralities were realistic. Spenser and Shakespeare were romantic; Jonson classical and realistic. The Elizabethan drama was largely romantic; even Seneca's influence, except in point of form, was such. The seventeenth century was clearly transitional. The romantic and the classical were balanced in Milton. In Donne the realistic predominated over the other two tendencies. Meantime in Dryden and the Restoration Comedy the approach to the "classical"

Introduction

became ever closer. Then the Augustan age entered in state under Pope and Addison and Johnson. Its prose was truly classical; its poetry was often pseudo-classical; yet the work of Collins and Gray struck a mean. Finally, realism was continued in a marked manner in the poetry of Crabbe and the prose of the novelists Fielding and Smollett.

In the nineteenth century romanticism and realism predominated: they are at the basis of the English genius; but classicism, in its old form of the Latin influence, and in its new form of the Greek, has had its large function; a function which it is the purpose of the present essay to summarize and estimate.

Bibliography

1. WALTER PATER: *Appreciations,* 1889. The *Postscript* discusses classicism and romanticism and their fusion in the greatest art.
2. WILLIAM DARNELL MCCLINTOCK: *Some Paradoxes of the English Romantic Movement (Chicago Decennial Publications,* vol. VII, pp. 341-347). Contains a valuable summary of the English romantic movement.
3. GEORGES PELLISSIER: *The Literary Movement in France in the Nineteenth Century,* translated by A. G. Brinton, 1897; Introduction and chapter on the Evolution of Realism.
4. P. BERGER: *William Blake, Poet and Mystic,* translated by Daniel H. Conner, 1914. The Introduction contains an excellent account of classicism and romanticism in France and England.
5. PAUL SHOREY: *Classical Literature and Learning (Congress of Arts and Sciences,* vol. III, p. 383, St. Louis, 1904; published in 1906.) A brilliant survey of the influence of Greece and Rome on mediaeval, Renaissance and modern times.
6. SANDYS: *A History of Classical Scholarship,* vols. I and II, 1906 and 1908. Invaluable for its record of Greek and Latin during the Middle Ages and the Renaissance.
7. F. G. TUCKER: *The Foreign Debt of English Literature,* 1907, chs. I and II, *Greek Literature and English* and *Latin Literature and English.*
8. J. CHURTON COLLINS: *Greek Influence on English Poetry,* 1910.

II
The Romantic Revolt

As a boy Coleridge was an inspired Grecian;[9] as a man he turned more and more towards the Gothic,[10] losing himself finally in German romantic methaphysics. Yet his *The Friend, Table Talk, Lectures on Shakespeare, Lectures on Literature,* and *Biographia Literaria* are filled with classical matters and show a remarkable range of interest in mediaeval as well as ancient writings. In his *Anima Poetae* he tells of a plan to make a catalogue of Greek and Latin authors, modern as well as classical. His poetry is romantic, with only rare classical references.—Wordsworth began as a romanticist of Nature and Human Nature and grew towards classicism,[11] less inspired by Plato,[12] Sappho, Alcaeus and Simonides[13] however, than by Virgil and Horace.[14] Ovid gave him a genuine feeling for mythology.[15] He was interested, too, in the classical archaeology of England,[16] Scotland,[17] France,[18] and Italy.[19]—William Godwin and his circle shared the eighteenth century's ad-

[9] Charles Lamb: "Christ's Hospital Thirty-five Years Ago."
[10] "Lectures on Shakespeare," etc., II and XIV.
[11] Prof. J. W. Tupper: "The Growth of the Classical in Wordsworth's Poetry." ("Sewanee Review," vol. XXIII, pp. 95-107, Jan. 1915.)
[12] See his preface to "I Heard, (Alas!) 'Twas Only in a Dream" and to his "Ode on Intimations of Immortality."
[13] Yet see "Upon the Same Occasion," ("September, 1819") for references to these three Greek lyric poets.
[14] "Memorials of a Tour in Italy," I; and "Liberty."
[15] Preface to his "Ode to Lycoris."
[16] Sonnet II (1835), "Roman Antiquities Discovered at Bishopstone, Herefordshire;" also note to "The River Duddon," XVII, "Return."
[17] "Yarrow Revisited, and Other Poems," XXVI, "The Broach."
[18] "Memorials of a Tour on the Continent," XXXIV.
[19] "Memorials of a Tour in Italy."

miration of the Romans as models of virtue and liberty.[20]—Shelley early adopted the rationalism, socialism and atheism of Godwin,[21] but later turned to the Greeks, assimilating with avidity for his purposes the Plato[22] of the *Ion* and the *Symposium*, the tragedians, Bion and Moschus, and, in a lesser degree, other ancients, mediaevalists and moderns, but showing especial genius in his use of mythology.[23]—Thomas Love Peacock satirized the Romantic group in a series of novelettes; was influential in turning Shelley from Godwinism to Greek;[24] and counted among his own favorite writers Aristophanes, Lucian, Apuleius, Nonnus and Tacitus.[25] But his *Maid Marian* and *The Misfortunes of Elphin* are romantic.—Keats valued Latin chiefly as a key to mediaeval lore;[26] Greek he did not know; mythology he used with lavish hand, drawing it from Lemprière's *Dictionary*, Tooke's *Pantheon*, Spence's *Polymetis*[27] and English poetry. A Hellenistic poet, not a Hellenist, his "Greek Spirit" is too Alexandrian for Landor,[28] who says Keats' style is "extremely far removed from the boundaries of Greece." A growing sense of form in his poetry, however, is pointed out by William Vaughn Moody.[29]—Byron professed an admiration for Pope[30] and therefore for Horace's *Ars Poetica* and Aristotle's *Poetics;* cared noth-

[20] "Of the Study of the Classics" ("The Enquirer," Essay VI).
[21] Leslie Stephen: "Godwin and Shelley" ("Hours in a Library," vol. III).
[22] Oliver Elton: "A Survey of English Literature, 1780-1830," vol. II.
[23] Francis Thompson: "Shelley;" Vida D. Scudder: "The Greek Spirit in Shelley and Browning."
[24] Richard Garnett: "Thomas Love Peacock." ("Essays of an Ex-Librarian," p. 256.)
[25] See Garnett's, Freeman's and Van Doren's writings on Peacock.
[26] "Letters."
[27] Cambridge ed. of Keats, p. XVI; Colvin, "John Keats," p. 10.
[28] "Letters and Unpublished Writings of Walter Savage Landor," edited by Stephen Wheeler, p. 172.
[29] "A History of English Literature," pp. 296-7.
[30] Letter to John Murray, Sept. 15, 1817.

The Classical Influence in English Literature

ing for Plato;[31] and had his fling at classical writers generally in *Don Juan*. He early mourned the departed glories of antiquity in *Childe Harold*, and his last three months were spent at Missolonghi, serving the Greeks.—Southey is more admired to-day for his character than for eminence as a writer or scholar. He knew Greek and Latin after a fashion, but used them little: instead he mastered Portuguese and Spanish. But one classical author he kept constantly by him; namely, the Stoic Epictetus.[32]

---

[31] Sept. 3, 1811: "I am no Platonist; I am nothing at all."
[32] "D. N. B;" also Edward Dowden's Life of Southey.

III

Major Prose Writers, Exclusive of the Novelists

CHAPMAN'S *Odyssey* was the basis of Lamb's *Adventures of Ulysses*;[33] and a desire to read Milton entire, even to his Latin, turned him again to that tongue.[34] He admired and translated in part the Latin poems of Vincent Bourne. He received much benefit from C. A. Elton's *Specimens of the Classic Poets,* — expressing himself as especially pleased with Hesiod.[35]—Hazlitt wrote *On Classical Education,* in *The Round Table,* No. 2, holding that the Classics are not primarily important because they strengthen the intellect, but because they soften and refine the taste. He himself knew Latin and French, but not Greek.[36]—De Quincey owed some of the eloquence of his impassioned prose to Cicero.[37] He wrote many essays on classical subjects. He divided human intellectual energy into two hemispheres, Greek and Christian.[38] In his *Brief Appraisal of the Greek Literature in Its Foremost Pretensions,* however, he held that Greek literature is overrated; that one can get most of it in translation or a substitute for it in Shakespeare and Milton.—Landor took his stand on Rome and looked backward to Greece and forward to modern times through the Middle Ages and the Renaissance. By means of verse and prose dialogues and letters of much restraint and beauty he made each of these ages live again.

[33] See his "Preface;" also his "Letters."
[34] Letter to Coleridge, Oct. 23, 1802.
[35] Letter to C. A. Elton, Aug. 12, 1821.
[36] "Dictionary of National Biography."
[37] Mackail: "A History of Latin Literature," p. 71.
[38] "Letters to a Young Man Whose Education Has Been Neglected," III.

The Classical Influence in English Literature

As a scholar he was fond of *minutiae:* as a critic he delivered independent judgments unfavorable to Plato and favorable to Greek and Roman lyric and elegy, to Homer, Aristotle, and Epicurus, Virgil, Horace, and others.[39]— Macaulay's classical reading is one of the phenomena of the century: the more so because his *Lays of Ancient Rome,* his letters, and his early contributions to *Knight's Magazine,* namely his *Scenes from Athenian Revels* and *Fragments of a Roman Tale,* — alone attest that amazing knowledge; if we except, of course, the occasional classical references in his speeches and essays.[40]—Carlyle wrote appreciatively of Greek and Latin in his History of Literature and embodied the spirit of Homer and the Greek tragedians in his *French Revolution.*[41]—Newman's master of style was Cicero, and his favorite ancient philosopher was Plato. His *Callista* is laid in Alexandria. He was a modern Alexandrian himself, showing, like the Alexandrians, distinct strains of Hellenism, Judaism and Christianity.[42] — Matthew Arnold preached Culture to the Victorian age and pointed out the proportionate claims of the Hellenic, Hebraic and Celtic spirits.[43] He was saturated with Homer.[44] His *Essays in Criticism, First Series,* contains a paper on Marcus Aureli-

---

[39] Wm. Chislett, Jr.: "Walter Savage Landor and His Relation to the Classical Tradition in English Literature." (Master's Thesis, Stanford University, May, 1912.)

[40] George Otto Trevelyan: "Life and Letters of Lord Macaulay;" "Marginal Notes of Lord Macaulay." Wm. Chislett, Jr: "Macaulay's Classical Reading" ("Classical Journal," XI, 142-150.)

[41] Helen C. Flint: "Indications in Carlyle's 'French Revolution' of the Influence of Homer and the Greek Tragedians" ("Classical Journal", vol. 5, pp. 118-126.)

[42] "D. N. B."

[43] See especially his "Culture and Anarchy."

[44] See his "Essay on Translating Homer," his poems "The New Sirens," "The Strayed Reveller" and "Palladium;" Prof. Milo G. Derham's "Borrowings and Adaptations from the 'Iliad' and 'Odyssey' in Matthew Arnold's 'Sohrab and Rustum' " ("University of Colorado Studies," 1909, vol. 7. pp. 73-89); and Prof. W. P. Mustard's "Homeric Echoes in Arnold's Balder Dead" ("Studies in Honor of Basil L. Gildersleeve," 19-28.)

us and a study of *Pagan and Religious Sentiment,* in which he translates the Fifteenth Idyl of Theocritus. In *A Speech at Eton* he defends the classics. In *On the Modern Element in Literature (Essays in Criticism, Third Series),* he shows in a general way the modernity of the age of Pericles and of Rome. His *Notebooks* include a large number of Greek and Latin quotations.[45]—Ruskin had a strong personal bent towards mediaevalism and modernism, but a clear conception of the aesthetic and historical values of Classicism. He had a good working knowledge of Greek and Roman writers. In the Greeks, at their best, he saw a desire to act rightly in art and conduct: he was impatient with the view that Beauty was their primary aim. In Rome he saw order and law. For ethical values he preferred Hebraism and Christianity, and was never tired of pointing out the evolution of things ancient into things modern; of things pagan into things Christian.[46]—In Pater aestheticism and asceticism found embodiment in such classical writers as Apuleius and Plato; yet he saw a strain of the Platonic in Apuleius, and of the Apuleian in Plato.[47] He declared that in perfect art romanticism and classicism are balanced, and he pointed out both elements in ancient, Renaissance and modern art.[48]—Wilde renounced Ruskin as "ethical always," defended impulse and unrestraint and

---

[45] In his "Early Poems" classical influence other than Homeric is shown in "A Modern Sappho," "Mycerinus" (based on Horodotus) and "Horatian Echo;" in "Lyric Poems," in "Fragment of an 'Antigone,'" "Fragment of Chorus of a 'Dejaneira,'" "Philomela," "Urania," "Euphrosyne," "Bacchanalia; or the New Age," "Thyrsus," (for mythology, which Arnold uses rarely); in "Dramatic Poems," in "Merope" (Apollodorus and Hyginus) and "Empedocles on Aetna."

[46] The index volume (XXXIX) of Cook and Wedderburn's great Library Edition of Ruskin's Works, 1903-12, is indispensable for the student of the classical or any other aspect of Ruskin's genius. See, for example, under "Greece," "Rome," "Homer," "Plato," "Xenophon" and "Virgil."

[47] "Marius the Epicurean" and "Plato and Platonism."

[48] See especially "The Renaissance" and "Appreciations."

The Classical Influence in English Literature

called his Individualism, New Hellenism. He carried Pater's and Whistler's Art for Art's Sake theories to an extreme, fused the terms romantic and classical, and lived and wrote for Beauty and Pleasure unrestrained.[49]

---

[49] Wm. Chislett, Jr.: "The New Hellenism of Oscar Wilde." ("Sewanee Review," July, 1915.) Reprinted in the present volume.

IV

Major Victorian Poets

TENNYSON has been called "the English Virgil." He considered Homer the greatest of poets and was steeped in Greek lyric, Theocritus, Lucretius, Catullus, Virgil, and Horace. He absorbed the styles of these poets and imbedded them in his own poetry. His allusions to classical history and mythology are numerous. He chose among classical subjects themes before but imperfectly treated, and gave them a modern tone.[50]—In *The Dead Pan* Mrs. Browning celebrated the victory of Christ over the pagan gods. Yet as a young girl she wrote *The Battle of Marathon* in imitation of Pope. She was learned in Greek. Her enthusiasm for the tragedians and Plato is set forth in *The Wine of Cyprus*. Her translation of the *Prometheus Bound* is probably the best verse rendering of the tragedy in English. She also translated from Homer, Hesiod, Euripides, Anacreon, Theocritus, Bion, Apuleius and Nonnus. Pindar, Aristophanes, Sappho, and notably Lucretius, are praised in *A Vision of Poets;* also Homer, the Greek tragedians, Hesiod, Theocritus and Virgil. Her interest in the liberation of Italy is shown in *Casa Guidi Windows*.—The perfection of classical art[51] did not appeal strongly to

---

[50] For the classical in Tennyson see especially Prof. W. P. Mustard's "Classical Echoes in Tennyson," supplemented by Prof. Curtis C. Bushnell's "Some New Material Dealing with the Classical Influence on Tennyson," in "The Proceedings of the American Philological Association," 40. XXII-V. See also Miss Elizabeth H. Haight's "Tennyson's Use of Homeric Material" ("Poet-Lore," XII, 541-551); Hallam Tennyson's "Alfred Lord Tennyson, a Memoir by His Son," vol. II, and T. G. Tucker's "The Foreign Debt of English Literature," (passim).

[51] For the classical in Browning see Mrs. Orr's "Handbook," G. W. Cooke's "Guide-Book to the Poetic and Dramatic Works of Robert Browning,"

The Classical Influence in English Literature

Browning, who was a modern and a mediaevalist. The romantic Aeschylus, Euripides and Aristophanes interested him more than the classical Sophocles; and Ovid rather than Virgil. He translated the *Agamemnon* and the *Herakles;* and paraphrased the *Alcestis* in *Balaustion's Adventure.* An extraordinary knowledge of Aristophanes is displayed in his *Aristophanes' Apology.*—Rossetti received a fair classical education and was interested in later life in Homer, Virgil, the history of Rome, *Gesta Romanorum* and St. Augustine.[52] Both in his poetry and painting he treated classical subjects romantically. Christina Rosetti knew Homer, temperamentally, at second hand, through her brothers and sister and a haze of modern world-weariness. She is both finely Greek and exquisitely English, however, in her lyrical *Venus's Looking-Glass.*—Morris included Homer and Hesiod among his "bibles"; called Herodotus, Plato, Aeschylus, Sophocles, Aristophanes, Theocritus, Lucretius, and Catullus *real* ancient imaginative works;[53] enjoyed Plutarch's *Lives* and Holland's *Pliny* and rejected Milton for his "cold classicalism and Puritanism."[54] Morris was the

the "Letters of Robert Browning and Elizabeth Barrett," Wm. Cranston Lawton's "The Classical Element in Browning's Poetry" ("Boston Browning Society Papers"), Vida D. Scudder's "The Greek Spirit in Shelley and Browning," ("Boston Society Papers," 1897), C. C. Bushnell's, "A Study of Browning's 'Agamemnon,'" ("Proceedings of the American Philological Association," vol. 32, pp. xcvii-xcix), Philip Stafford Moxon's, "Balaustion's Opinion of Euripides," ("Boston Society Papers"), Prof. R. G. Moulton's "Balaustion's Adventure as a Beautiful Misrepresentation of the Original," ("Boston Society Papers") and Dr. Carl Newall Jackson's "Classical Elements in Browning's 'Aristophanes' Apology,'" ("Harvard Studies in Classical Philology," vol. XX)," reviewed by Professor Gildersleeve in the "American Journal of Philology," 1910, vol. 31, pp. 487-9.

[52] For the Rossettis, see W. M. Rossetti's "Letters and Memoir of Dante Gabriel Rossetti."

[53] Though not including Virgil in these categories, he translated his "Aeneids," in which he was interested, according to Mackail, in his "Life of Morris," as "the fountain-head of romanticism in European literature."

[54] For the list of fifty-four titles which Morris sent to the "Pall Mall Gazette," in 1885, as his "Best Hundred Books," see May Morris' Introduction to vol. XXII of her father's works.

greatest story-teller of the century; he was a mediaeval romancer with much of the clarity and sense of the ancient and modern world. His classical stories, *The Life and Death of Jason*,[55] *The Earthly Paradise* and *Scenes from the Fall of Troy* are clothed in mediaeval imagery. Landor dealt with antiquity as a classicist; Morris as a mediaevalist; Tennyson as a modernist. —Another modernist, though often called a Grecian, and though professing to follow Landor in all things—Algeron Charles Swinburne—went back for inspiration in his early work to the later Greek decadence. Both in prose and in poetry he frequently wrote in excess. His mastery of classical and modern verse forms, however, was complete. In his later work Swinburne became a "romantic humanitarian";[56] a poet-laureate of Liberty,—English, French, Russian and Italian.[57] Swinburne's literary gods were Aeschylus, Sappho ("the greatest poet that ever lived"),[58] Pindar, Catullus, Shakespeare, Landor, Hugo and Mazzini. His demi-gods were Homer, Sophocles, Euripides, Marlowe, Jonson, Richard Burton, Blake, Coleridge, Shelley, the Brontës and the Rossettis.

---

[55] See H. Sybil Kermode's "The Classical Sources of Morris's Life and Death of Jason." ("Primitiae," The University of Liverpool, 1912).
[56] The "Nation," vol. 97, p. 510. [57] See his Odes.
[58] Swinburne: "Sappho" ("Living Age," 280, 817-18).

V
The Novelists

MARIA EDGEWORTH knew Italian and French, a little Latin and no Greek. In his *Practical Education* (in which his daughter had some hand) R. L. Edgeworth (ch. XIII, *Grammar and Classical Literature*) advocated emphasis on translation of Latin, with only a half hour a day expended on Grammar.—Scott was fond of Latin poetry;[59] used Latin phrases, especially in *The Fortunes of Nigel* and *The Antiquary;* commented on the Greek Drama in his *Essay on the Drama,* and echoed Homēr, through Pope, in his heroic poetry, especially in *Marmion.*[60]—Jane Austen reacted against the Gothic romance,[61] and wrote six realistic novels of the best type showing distinct traces of her knowledge of French.—Charlotte and Emily Brontë also knew French, together with a little Latin from their father. Emily's *Wuthering Heights* has been compared to Greek tragedy,[62] but is lacking in restraint; a quality on the other hand, which characterizes most of her exceedingly subjective poetry.—Miss Mitford is still read for her *Our Village:* among her dramas *Rienzi* was successful.—Mrs. Gaskell's books show fineness and poise, especialy her *Cranford* and *Cousin Phillis.*—Thackeray's favorite Latin writer was Horace, with Virgil a close second; he also knew and quoted frequently Juvenal, Ovid, Lucretius, and Christian

---

[59] "Dictionary of National Biography."
[60] J. C. Shairp: "The Homeric Spirit in Walter Scott." ("Aspects of Poetry").
[61] In "The Mystery, an Unfinished Comedy;" "Northanger Abbey" and "Sense and Sensibility."
[62] May Sinclair: "The Three Brontës," p. 251.

Latin.[63] His style has the fineness and precision of the best classical prose writing of the eighteenth century, with a warmth and flexibility of its own, more Greek than Latin, if anything, yet drawing almost nothing directly from Greek. He caught the Greek spirit when he visited the Parthenon; he did not get it when in school, owing, he says, to unsympathetic and cruel masters.[64]—Dickens satirized the pedantic teaching of Latin, Greek, mathematics and science of his day.[65] He had some slight knowledge of Caesar, Cicero, Virgil, Horace and Livy,[66] used a few Latin phrases and traveled in Italy, recording his impressions with discrimination, but with little enthusiasm.[67]—George Eliot's scholarship was extensive.[68] She read widely in the classics and criticized translations as substitutes for the originals.[69] Her archaeology, Roman and Florentine, was conscientious and weighty; to some, uninspired.[70] She wrote discriminatingly on Mythology,[71] and used gods and goddesses and their trains for artistic purposes;[72] yet she never rose to Meredith's heights of mythological metaphor. Like Dickens she mentions Latin as an English school, or rather University, subject. But her attitude is different; for whereas he labored to teach England to present Latin and other subjects pleasantly,[73] she speaks banteringly of

[63] Rachel R. Hiller: "Thackeray's Knowledge of Latin." (Master's Thesis, Stanford University, May, 1907.)
[64] "A Journey from Cornhill to Cairo," ch. V, on Athens.
[65] James L. Hughes: "Dickens as an Educator."
[66] See his "Our School." [67] "Pictures from Italy."
[68] See Oscar Browning's, G. W. Cooke's, J. W. Cross's, Leslie Stephen's and W. C. Brownell's Lives and studies of George Eliot.
[69] "The Lifted Veil."
[70] G. W. Cooke: "George Eliot, a Critical Study." Leslie Stephen: "George Eliot."
[71] In a review of Mackay's "Progress of the Intellect" ("Westminster Review," Jan. 18, 1851).
[72] "Poems."
[73] J. L. Hughes: "Dickens as an Educator."

Latin (in character) as an adjunct to a gentleman, and as one means of affording a girl masculine understanding.[74] But on the whole her women, unlike Meredith's, are Ariadnes, not Minervas. Among men, she draws Mr Irwine, a gentle Epicurean, Mr. Brooke, a dilettante, Mr. Casaubon, a pedant, and Bardo, Scala and Politian, Renaissance scholars.[75] Tito is a subtle, faunlike, treacherous creature; Romola is George Eliot's self,—Italian, English, Christian, Greek.—Bulwer-Lytton reacted against Byronic pose.[76] In a classical way, he was acquainted with the chief Greek and Latin writers and made Pompeii live in his *Last Days of Pompeii*. In addition, he wrote *Rienzi*, translated the *Odes* and *Epodes* of Horace and left unfinished a *History of Athens* and *Pausanias the Spartan*, a romance.—His son, Edward Robert Bulwer-Lytton ("Owen Meredith") won fame with his *Lucile*. Richard Garnett has compared his life to that of an Elizabethan noble's.[77] His interest in philosophy and religion caused him to read Plato, Aristotle and Epictetus.[78] His poem *Marah* shows a mingling of the Christian and pagan spirits.—Disraeli wrote two Lucianic burlesques,—*Ixion in Heaven* and *The Infernal Marriage*. In the former Byron is satirized as Apollo; in the latter English high life is ridiculed. In *Tancred*, ch. LII, Disraeli paints a glowing picture of Anserey, a land north of Antioch, to which Queen Astarte has fled to keep alive the ancient worship of the gods.—In this Autobiography, Anthony Trollope expresses a fondness for Latin Literature. He became interested in Caesar and Augustus and wrote two articles on them in the *Dublin University Magazine*. Later he published his *Commentaries of Caesar* and his *Life*

[74] "Adam Bede," "The Mill on the Floss," "The Lifted Veil," "Romola," "Felix Holt," "Middlemarch."
[75] "Adam Bede," "Middlemarch," "Romola."
[76]. In "Pelham," 1828.   [77] "D. N. B."
[78] See his "Letters."

of Cicero.—Kingsley gave his idea of the causes of the barbarian attack on Rome in his *Roman and Teuton*. Among his poems are *Andromeda* and *Sappho*. His interest in Alexandrianism found expression in *Alexandria and Her Scholars (Historical Lectures and Essays)*, and in his novel *Hypatia*, which deals with the conflict between Paganism and Christianity. In all his books Kingsley advocated intellectual moderation and physical energy.—Charles Reade retained a fellowship at Magdalen College, Oxford, till his death, but spent most of his time in London.[79] His *The Cloister and the Hearth* is laid in the period of the German Renaissance and is a learned book as well as a good story: his other novels and sketches also show his fondness for Latin.—Wilkie Collins' *Antonina* was the outcome of two or three years in Italy and of a boyish admiration for Bulwer-Lytton.[80] His later work was marred by melodrama; but his *Woman in White* is much read.—Stevenson was a realistic romanticist who appreciated Homer, caught the Greek spirit, praised Latin for its conciseness, knew Roman Law, imitated Cicero, quoted Virgil and Horace, admired Martial and called Petronius "silly stuff."[81]—Mrs Lynn Linton was the "anti-suffragette" leader of her day; but before embarking upon her studies of the modern girl, she wrote *Amymone, a Romance of the Days of Pericles*, 3 vols., 1848.—Blackmore's favorite poets were Homer, Virgil, Milton and Matthew Arnold. In 1862 he translated the first and second *Georgics* of Virgil under the title of *The Farm and Fruit of Old*. *Lorna Doone* (1869) led a romantic revolt against the novel of manners.[82]—Sir Walter Besant improved conditions in East London by writing *All Sorts and Conditions of Men*. He was at one time Professor in the

[79] "D. N. B."   [80] "D. N. B."
[81] Wm. Chislett, Jr.: "Stevenson and the Classics" ("Journal of English and Germanic Philology," vol. XV, April, 1916.)
[82] "D. N. B."

The Classical Influence in English Literature

Royal College of Mauritius. Traces of his classical reading may be detected in his novels. Among his descriptive books on London, the volume on *Early London* devotes Chapters I - IV to the Roman occupation.—George Gissing wrote a clear classical style and amused himself when not at work on his gloomy novels by studying Greek metres and in reading Classics in the British Museum. He also drew consolation from Marcus Aurelius.[83] In *By the Ionian Sea* he has recorded his impressions of Southern Italy.—As "Fiona Macleod" William Sharp was a Celtic romanticist. He planned a volume to be called *Greek Backgrounds*— "to deal with the ancient (recreated) and modern backgrounds of some of the greatest of the Greeks," according to Mrs. Sharp.[84]—George Meredith preached temperance and the mean through comedy, conformity to nature, and sane relations between men and women.[85] He praised Homer,[86] attacked the philosophy of Horace, was interested in Aristophanes, and especially appreciated Menander through Terence.[87] He admired the French, notably Molière. His classical metaphors are numerous and poetical.—The classical influence on Thomas Hardy is literary, archaeological and anthropological on the Roman side, and literary and philosophical on the Greek. The Roman ruins of his native Dorchester, Rome herself, Sophocles in his submission to Fate, and Aeschylus in Promethean revolt against it, are his chief sources of ancient inspiration.—In *Robert Elsmere* Mrs. Humphrey Ward refers to Aeschylus, Cato, Ovid,

---

[83] Morley Roberts: "The Private Life of Henry Maitland."

[84] In her "William Sharp, a Memoir," ch. XXIV. See ch. XI for Sharp's interest in Rome.

[85] See G. M. Trevelyan: "The Poetry and Philosophy of George Meredith;" also Meredith's "Essay on Comedy," "The Egoist" and "To the Comic Spirit."

[86] Letter to Arthur Meredith, Dec. 16, 1871.

[87] "An Essay on Comedy."

Virgil, Livy and Justinian.[88]—George Moore published *Pagan Poems* in 1881 and *Hail and Farewell: Ave, Salve, Vale*, in 1911, 1912, and 1914. Though formerly a follower of the French naturalists he is now usually identified with the Celtic school.—There are references to Homer, Virgil and Horace in Kipling's verse,[89] and to the Romans in Britain in *Puck o' Pook's Hill*.—H. G. Wells read Plato late in life and recommends the study of Greek generally.[90]—Maurice Hewlett, May Sinclair and Eden Phillpott's have more than a touch of the pagan spirit. Phillpott's *Wild Fruit*—a volume of excellent verse—is full of it.—Among Hewlett's poems is *Helen Redeemed*. His last novel, at this writing, is *The Little Iliad*.—Sir Arthur Quiller-Couch's enthusiasm for the Classics is expressed in his *The Art of Writing*, 1916.

For completeness, the reader is referred to *The Cambridge History of English Literature*, vol. XII, ch. XI, and vol. XIII, ch. XIII, *Lesser Novelists*. The bibliographies to these chapters are lengthy but relatively unimportant for our purposes here. But note especially J. Henry Shorthouse (1834-1903) whose *John Inglesant* discloses its author's knowledge of Plato, Aristophanes, Lucretius and Terence.

---

[88] J. Stuart Walters: "Mrs. Humphrey Ward," ch. III.
[89] Thomas K. Sidey: "Echoes from the Classics in Kipling." ("Modern Language Notes," vol. 24, p. 217).
[90] Van Wyck Brooks: "The World of H. G. Wells," 1915, p. 14.

VI

Minor Writers

KIRKE WHITE was a romanticist who knew his Classics; he was edited by Southey and praised by Byron;[91] his poetry celebrates Nature, Religion and the Feelings.—Mrs. Hemans is best known for her poems of the affections, but enthusiasm for Greece, ancient and modern, is shown in such verses as her *Modern Greece* and her Greek songs.— Praed was a good Latinist at school and college, and his *vers de société* shows classical restraint.—Campbell made short translations from Tyrtaeus, Alcman and Euripides and wrote a *Song of the Greeks.*—Hood's classical poems are *Lamia, Hero and Leander* and *Lycus the Centaur.*— Sydney Smith disparaged grammar and gerund-grinding as the best method of acquiring knowledge of the classics. He advocated translations, interlinear, literal, and free, and criticized the classical curriculum of his day as stimulating imagination rather than reasoning power."[92]—Isaac D'Israeli's *Curiosities of Literature* includes notes on *Cicero's Puns, Aristotle and Plato, Modern Platonism* and *Ancient and Modern Saturnalia.*—Hartley Coleridge's poetry and prose are marked by grace, refinement, and restraint. He read and recommended minor as well as major classical writers.[93]—Beddoes read Greek and used mythology with imaginative power; but his true affinity was for Elizabethan and Senecan tragedy.[94]—Francis Jeffrey had a good lit-

---

[91] "English Bards and Scotch Reviewers," 831-48; also Letter to Dallas, Aug. 27, 1811.

[92] See his essays on "Professional Education" and on "Hamilton's Method of Teaching Languages," ("Edinburgh Review," 1809 and 1826, vols. 15 and 44).

[93] "Memoirs of Roger Ascham." [94] "The Bride's Tragedy."

erary knowledge of the classics.—Thomas Moore read omnivorously, and his footnotes show that he was thoroughly familiar with the classical writers, major and minor. And with all his learning he preserved deftness of touch. In addition to his *Odes of Anacreon,* Moore translated a few poems from the Greek Anthology, imitated Catullus and Martial, and paraphrased Horace. Peacock criticised unfavorably his prose romance, *The Epicurean. Rhymes on the Road* deal with modern Italy.—Nature, religion, war, and politics are Montgomery's subjects. He knew something of Italian, a little Greek, and Latin.—"Christopher North" was an authority on the Greek Anthology and wrote on *The Agamemnon of Aeschylus* and *Homer and his Translations* in his *Essays Critical and Imaginative.*— Samuel Rogers published a long poem *Italy,* to supplement *Childe Harold.* He refers to Horace and Virgil in other places and translates a fragment of Euripides and a Greek epigram.—Lemprière's Classical Dictionary was a favorite book of Leight Hunt,[95] whose poems include *Hero and Leander,* four translations from Homer, two from Theocritus, two from Anacreon, two from the *Anthology* and one each from Catullus and Martial. He was not above reading translations.[96] He was fond of Anacreon, Theocritus, Virgil and Ovid. His style has the good form and the grace of the best in classicism and romanticism.—Clough revised Dryden's translation of Plutarch's *Lives.* He used Greek and Latin phrase titles and experimented in classical metres.—Bryan Waller Proctor's *Julian the Apostate* and *The Rape of Proserpine* show dependence on Gibbon and Greek tragedy, respectively.—Sydney Dobell's *The Roman, a Dramatic Poem,* is concerned with the Ital-

[95] "Dictionary of National Biography."
[96] "Scholarship and No Scholarship," (in "The Seer").

The Classical Influence in English Literature

ian struggle for liberty.—Robert Stephen Hawker lived in Cornwall, where he wrote much good romantic poetry. At Oxford he won the Newdigate prize with a poem on Pompeii.—As a literary man Bagehot is perhaps best known for his essay *Wordsworth, Tennyson and Browning; or Pure, Ornate and Grotesque Art in English Poetry.*—In 1835 George Borrow published *Targum*, a series of translations from thirty languages and dialects. How he learned Lilly's Latin Grammar by heart in three years is set forth in the sixth chapter of *Lavengro.*—Arthur O'Shaughnessy's poetry is influenced throughout by French romanticism.— In *The City of Dreadful Night* James Thomson follows Heraclitus in declaring "Naught is constant on the earth but change." His *Modern Penelope* and *Siren's Song* show the influence of the *Odyssey.*—FitzGerald began his work on Omar by turning him into Latin.[97] His *Agamemnon* is an adaptation of the original, written to "popularize a great play;" his *Downfall and Death of King Oedipus*, is, by his own admission, merely a paraphrase.[98] His *Euphranor* is modeled on the Platonic dialogues, and his English boys carry on Greek talk delightfully. After reading his *Letters*, Meredith declared his taste in the classics quite sound, and infantile out of them. The *Letters* are indeed an extraordinary record of classical appreciation.—Charles Stuart Calverley translated Theocritus and portions of Homer into English, turned numerous English poems into Latin, wrote on the theory of translation and produced considerable original verse.[99]—Lord Houghton's *Memoirs* contain recollections of Landor and other friends. His prose writing also includes a paper on

---

[97] Edmund Gosse: "The Complete Works of Edward Fitzgerald," vol. I, pp. XVIII-XIX. [98] See his "Letters."
[99] See "The Complete Works of C. S. Calverley," edited by Sir Walter J. Sendall, London, Bell and Sons, 1910.

The Classical Influence in English Literature

The Present Social Results of Classical Education in F. W. Farrar's *Essays on a Liberal Education*. Among his poems, his *Memorials of Travels in Greece and Italy* show his enthusiasm for both countries, ancient and modern.— Like Landor, Richard Jefferies saw that feminine element in the Greek genius[1] which Pater resolutely excluded. Jefferies acquired Classics through translations. In this way he read Diogenes Laertius, Plato, Aristotle, Athenaeus and Sophocles.[2] He was interested in Greek sculpture and numismatics.—In *"A Thing of Beauty Is a Joy Forever"* Eliza Cook declares "No yellow wave of Pactolus" supplies motive power to her humble poems. *Melaia*, however, is a romantic story laid "in the age when Arts and Peace revived once more in mighty Greece."—William Allingham was advised by Landor to learn Greek grammar before Latin, since the former "comprehends the latter and much more."[3] Clough advised him to regard Latin as living — a sort of ante-Dantean Italian.[4] His own writing is simple, graceful and clear. *Bona Dea* is a long address, for him, to Earth.—Symonds won high honors at Balliol. His chief work is his *Renaissance in Italy*. He was fond of such Alexandrians as Theocritus, and of later writers like Ausonius and Politian.[5] His *Wine, Women and Song* is a translation of mediaeval Latin student songs.—Frederick Locker-Lampson wrote graceful *vers de société*.—Lord de Tabley's *Philoctetes and Orestes* are poetical dramas influenced by Swinburne's *Atalanta*. His *Orpheus in Thrace* was published posthumously in 1901.—

---

[1] Edward Thomas: "Richard Jefferies, His Life and Works."
[2] "Nature and Books" (in "Field and Hedgerow").
[3] "Letters to William Allingham," ed. by H. Allingham and E. Baumer Williams, 1911, pp. 219-20.
[4] Id. p. 162.
[5] "Dictionary of National Biography." See also his "Studies of the Greek Poets."

The Classical Influence in English Literature

Coventry Patmore's Psyche Odes in his *Unknown Eros* are based on a favorite belief of his that the pagan myths contain the elements of Christian doctrine in symbol.[6]— T. E. Brown was a Manxman. His *Roman Women* is an intoxicated eulogy. In *Israel* and *Hellas* he balances the two nations to see which "went the straighter to its aim," but a decision is not reached.—Frederick Tennyson's poetry is of the best type of Landorian classicism. His *Isles of Greece* is based on fragments of Sappho and Alcaeus, and is said to present the characters of the poets with originality.—Grant Allen knew his Classics well[7] and translated the *Attis* and the *Ut Flos in Septis* of Catullus. His *The Return of Aphrodite* is a charming classical poem.—H. D. Traill shows his enthusiasm for Lucian in a study in his *The New Fiction and Other Essays on Literary Subjects*. Lucian, again, inspires his *The New Lucian, Being a Series of Dialogues of the Dead.*—Robert Buchanan's "pseudo-classic" poems, *Undertones*, were inspired by Peacock's verse, according to Buchanan himself, and deal with mythological themes.[8] Other classical poems are *Old Rome* and *The New Rome*.—Aubrey de Vere praised both Landor and Keats as Grecians,[9] and Landor, in turn, commended his *The Search after Proserpine*, 1843. In 1850 De Vere published *Picturesque Sketches of Greece and Turkey*. His *Urbs Roma* is a series of fifteen sonnets on modern Rome.[10] In his *Literature in Its Social Aspects (Essays Literary and Ethical)* he touched on Greek lyric poetry.— F. J. Bailey's *Festus* contains many classical references.— Samuel Butler wrote *The Authoress of the Odyssey*, delivered a lecture on *The Humour of Homer* and collaborated

---

[6] Edmund Gosse: "Coventry Patmore," p. 201.
[7] "Dictionary of National Biography."
[8] "Dictionary of National Biography."
[9] "Essays, Chiefly on Poetry."
[10] "D. N. B.," article "De Vere."

The Classical Influence in English Literature

with Henry Festing Jones in *Ulysses, an Oratorio*. He traveled widely in Greece and Italy.—William Ernest Henley appreciated Homer, Theocritus and Juvenal, though he knew little Greek or Latin. His poetry is romantic and realistic by turns: he was especially influenced by the French. As a critic he appreciated the several schools, pointing out carefully the merits and defects both of the romantic and the classical. Though temperamentally a fighter, his poetry and prose are usually marked by finish and restraint.—Ernest Dowson was influenced both by Latin and French.[11] His favorite among the ancients was Horace, whose influence on his poetry is marked. One-fourth of his poems have Latin titles.—In his *Post Liminium* Lionel Johnson shows wide reading and fine sympathy as a critic. In *The Classics* and in his *Lucretius* poems he celebrates his favorite classical authors. His poetry is usually characterized by restraint rather than emotion, but his *Ireland* and *To Morfydd* are vibrant with feeling.—Sir Edwin Arnold encloses one small poem, *Atalanta*, in his *Lotus and Jewel*. His *Translations from the Greek Poets* (in *Poems*, 1880), include passages from Homer, Hesiod, Simonides of Amorgos, Sappho, Anacreon, Mesomedes, Mimnermus, Theocritus, Bion and Proclus. The *Dictionary of National Biography* includes *The Poets of Greece*, 1869, and the *Hero and Leander* of Musaeus among his works.—Lafcadio Hearn was born in the Ionian Islands, of English and Greek parentage, lived in America for a time and died a Japanese citizen. His work has the restraint of his adopted people.—Sir Lewis Morris attempted in his *Epic of Hades* to retell the stories of Hellenic mythology with certain modern allegorical significance.

[11] See Arthur Symons' memoir prefixed to "The Poems of Ernest Dowson."

The Classical Influence in English Literature

Gycia: a Tragedy was based on Constantine Porphyrogenitus.—Francis Thompson read Blake and Aeschylus with ardor.[12] His essay *Paganism Old and New* holds that paganism with the Christian leaven in it is alone poetical.—John Davidson is known especially for his *Fleet Street Eclogues*. Among his plays *Scaramouch in Naxos* shows classical influence, with Ariadne, Bacchus, Silenus, satyrs and bacchantes engaging in the pantomine.—Andrew Lang was eminent as an anthropologist and took an active part in the Homeric controversy. With Leaf and Myers he translated the *Iliad*, and with Butcher, the *Odyssey*, into prose. He also translated the Homeric Hymns, Theocritus, Bion and Moschus. In his *Letters to Dead Authors* he writes to certain of the classic shades. His *Helen of Troy* — "a story in rhyme" — he based on Homer, Quintus Smyrnaeus and Euripides. His *Grass of Parnassus* contains some charming classical poems. — Alfred Austin's *A Tale of True Love and Other Poems*, 1902, includes *Polyphemus* and *In the Forum*, the latter a good "meditative" poem.—George Otto Trevelyan's *Interludes in Verse and Prose*, 1905, contains *An Ancient Greek War; Horace at the University of Athens; The Cambridge Dionysia, a Classic Dream*, filled with local Cambridge references; *The Modern Eccleziazusae, or Ladies in Parliament*, based on Aristophanes; and *Anglo-Indian Lyrics*, four of them imitations of Horace's *Odes*.—John Todhunter wrote an *Alcestis*, 1879, and a *Helen in Troas*, 1885.—Austin Dobson is a writer of *vers de société* and other light poetry of delicacy and charm. Horace is a prime favorite of his, and he translates or paraphrases him with felicity. His prose volumes — *Eighteenth Century Vignettes* and *Miscellanies*

---

[12] Everard Meynell: "The Life of Francis Thompson," pp. 58 and 90.

—show his affinity with the age of Pope,—especially with its minor and more romantic personalities.—Robert Bridges' work has classical restraint. Among his poems and plays are *Prometheus the Firegiver, Eros and Psyche, The Isle of Achilles, Achilles in Scyros, The Return of Ulysses, The History of Nero* and *The Feast of Bacchus.* He experiments with classical metres.—W. H. Mallock has written upon[13] and translated passages of Lucretius.[14] In his *The New Republic* he satirizes amiably a company of Victorian notables, including Pater, Arnold and Ruskin.— Edmund Gosse is influenced by Norway, France, Germany, Japan, and the England of Huxley and Arnold. His *Collected Poems,* 1911, show very considerable classical influence.—F. B. Money-Coutts' work has compression and careful technique. He published a *Psyche,* in 1911.—George Bernard Shaw has given his clever turn to classical stories in his *Androcles and the Lion* and in his *Pygmalion,* 1912. —In *Rome and Another* William Watson warns England against pride of power. He is noted for his epigrams. His *On Landor's Hellenics* summons men from the cloying sweetness of modern verse to the "bland Attic skies" of Landor.—George Russell ('A-E')'s paganism is that of earth worship.—Kenneth Grahame is the author of *Pagan Papers,* etc., and of a sketch, *The Roman Road,* in *The Yellow Book,* vol. II.—Arthur Symons praises the "calm rapture" of Robert Bridges. He himself is a romanticist whose beautiful lyrics savor of decadence. Of interest classically are his *Lesbia in Old Age* and his *From Catullus: Chiefly Concerning Lesbia* (in *The Knave of Hearts*).

---

[13] "Lucretius" in "Blackwood's Ancient Classics for English Readers," vol. 14, 1878.

[14] In his "Lucretius on Life and Death in the Metre of Omar Khayam," 1900.

The Classical Influence in English Literature

—Arthur Waugh and Hubert Crackanthorpe each contributed essays on *Reticence in Literature* to Volumes I and II, respectively, of *The Yellow Book*.—Richard Le Gallienne's *Book Bills of Narcissus* has a modern touch of the Greek spirit. His *Orestes, a Tragedy*, is based on Aeschylus. He is thoroughly conversant with French.—William Butler Yeats is a romanticist, and the leader of the Celtic movement, but in his *Ideas of Good and Evil* he writes appreciatively of Homer and of Robert Bridges' *The Return of Ulysses*.—Stephen Phillips published *Marpessa* and *Endymion* in 1896 and 1898. *Ulysses* and *Nero* appeared in 1902 and 1906.—Lawrence Binyon wrote *Penthesilea*, 1905, and *Paris and Oenone*, 1906.—In *Clio, a Muse*, George Macaulay Trevelyan advocates the classical conception of history as an Art as opposed to the modern notion of her as a Science.

(The following poets are added from Arthur Symons' *The Romantic Movement in English Poetry*.) William Gifford edited *Ben Jonson*, translated Juvenal and Persius and wrote *The Baviad* and *The Maeniad* to satirize writers of bad verse.—George Hookham Frere translated the *Frogs, Acharnians, Knights, Birds* and portions of the *Peace* of Aristophanes. His *Theognis Restitutus* aimed at an understanding of the personal history of the poet from existing fragments. Among his *Miscellaneous Translations* are renderings of Homer, Euripides, Empedocles, Catullus and Aesop. Other short translations and papers on classical subjects are contained in vol. I of his *Works*, Pickering, 1872.—Venus appears in person to deify James Hogg's *Russiade*.—Mrs. Tighe was the author of *Psyche, or the Legend of Love*, based on Apuleius's story.—In addition to his rendering of Dante, Cary translated Pindar, and the *Birds* of Aris-

The Classical Influence in English Literature

tophanes, 1824.—Dr. John Leyden was a remarkable linguist who wrote some imaginative poetry.—Horace Smith published in 1821 *Amarynthus* and *The Nympholept*, poems of fancy and sylvan charm.—Robert Eyres Landor collaborated with his brother Walter in translating the latter's *Gebir* into Latin. His *Fountain of Arethusa* is a fantastic romance peopled with dead Romans who had survived death and remained critics of the living.—Baron Thurlow published an *Ariadne* in 1814.—James Sheridan Knowles wrote *Caius Gracchus*, 1815, and *Virginius*, 1820. —Henry Hart Milman wrote *The Apollo Belvidere* and translated the *Agamemnon* and the *Bacchae*.—William Maginn invented a ballad metre for the translation of Homer and turned Lucian's dialogues into comedies in English blank verse.—Thomas Noon Talfourd wrote an *Ion* and *The Athenian Captives*.—John Hamilton Reynolds published his *The Naiad* in 1816.

(The following additional poets, showing classical influence, are taken from Miles' *The Poets and Poetry of the Century*.)—Edwin Atherstone based his *Last Days of Herculaneum*, 1821, on the account of the eruption of Vesuvius given by Pliny in his letter to Tacitus.—Richard Henry Horne issued *Orion, an Epic Poem in Three Books*, in 1843.—Among Richard Chevenix Trench's sonnets are two on *Vesuvius as Seen From Capri*.—Charles Tennyson Turner composed sonnets on *Orion, The Aeolian Harp* and *Alexander The Great's Designs at Babylon Frustrated*.— John Stuart Blackie translated Aeschylus and wrote on *Homer and The Iliad*.—Thomas Gordon Hake wrote *The Birth of Venus*, in twenty-nine stanzas.—Sir Francis Hastings Doyle was the author of *The Platonist, The Epicurean* and *Gythia*, a tale in verse of the lower Roman Empire. He published a translation of the *Oedipus Rex* in 1849.—

The Classical Influence in English Literature

A Glimpse of Italy records Alfred Domett's enthusiasm for that country.—Arthur Henry Hallam's *Scene at Rome* is a dialogue in verse between Raphael and Fiametta.— William James Linton's short lyric *The Epicurean* catches the ancient spirit.—In Thomas Westwood's *The Quest of the Sancgreall* appears his *The Legend of the Syren Isles*, combining Arthurian and classical legend.—Sir Joseph Noel Paton's *Amathea* is based on an epigram of Theon of Samos.—Dora Greenwell's *Demeter and Cora* records a conversation between Demeter and Proserpine.—Thomas Woolner was a sculptor who wrote a *Pygmalion* and a *Tiresias*.—Mortimer Collins wrote *A Greek Idyl* and *The Ivory Gate*.—Richard Watson Dixon was the author of *Apollo Pythius*.—Among John Nichol's works are *Mare Mediterraneum, The Death of Themistocles* and *Hannibal*, a play.—Richard Garnett wrote *Io in Egypt* and *Iphigenia in Delphi*. In 1869 he published *Idylls and Epigrams, Chiefly from the Greek Anthology*.—Among Thomas Ashe's later poems is *Lost Eros*.—Like Arnold, David Gray has verses on *Empedocles*.—Herman Charles Merivale wrote a poem of some length on *Old and New Rome*.—Madame Darmesteter is author of *The Crowned Hippolytus, The New Arcadia, An Italian Garden*, and *Etruscan Tombs*.— Mrs. Ernest Radford wrote an *Orpheus*.—Lionel Johnson praised Michael Field, a pseudonym for the Misses Bradley and Cooper, according to *Who's Who*, 1915. He says the lyrical poems of the volume *Long Ago* are suggested each by a fragment of Sappho. *Callirhöe* has charming faun scenes.—Alice Meynell's writing is noted for its fine restraint.

(Additional Minor Poets from F. St. John Corbett's *A History of English Poetry*, 1904).—William Sotheby translated the *Georgics* of Virgil in 1800, and the *Iliad* and

Odyssey in 1831-2.—Thomas Mitchell turned Aristophanes into English verse and edited some of the plays of Sophocles.—John Edmund Reade wrote *Catiline*, 1839 and *Italy*, which somewhat resembles *Childe Harold*.—The Rev. Henry Alford was author of *Chapters on the Greek Poets*.—The Rev. George Croly was author of *Verse Illustrations to Gems from the Antique*, and *Catiline*, a tragedy.

The reader is also referred to *The Cambridge History of English Literature*, vol. XII, ch. XIV, for writers on ancient history, and to ch. XV, for Sir John Edwin Sandys' account of the classical scholars and archaeologists of the century. See also vol. XIII, ch. VI, and Bibliography, for the following additional names and titles:—Arthur Gray Butler: *The Choice of Hercules;* Wathen Mack Wilks Call: *Lyra Hellenica;* George Augustus Simcox: *Prometheus Unbound;* the Earl of Derby: *Translations of Poems, Ancient and Modern;* Theodore Watts-Dunton: *Flowers of Parnassus;* Augusta Webster: *Prometheus Bound*, and the *Medea of Euripides;* Philip Stanhope Worsley: *The Temple of Janus* and *The Iliad of Homer;* and David Moir: *The Life of Mansie Wauch*, ch. 29, Conclusion.

VII

Conclusion

*Classicism in a Romantic Century.—The Greek Spirit.—
The Roman Spirit.*

IN an otherwise valuable volume on *Ruskin: A Study in Personality,* 1911, Mr. A. C. Benson makes some interesting statements regarding English classical education as applied to men of originality and genius of the last century. "Writers", says he, "must learn to express their thoughts in their own way; and it is better to borrow thoughts than to purloin a medium. The art of literary imitation is a very easy one, and needs only a very second-rate gift. Small wonder that we Englishmen, trained on so narrow a classical tradition, should be so prone to rank literary imitation high. Boys who have been taught that the best Latin verse and prose is the most ingenious cento of phrases, not imitated but transferred from classical writers, may be excused if they rank the gift of imitation above that of forcible expression. I mean to discuss the style of Ruskin elsewhere, but I hold that one of his supreme felicities was that his mind was not cramped by a classical education. I do not undervalue that education for other purposes; it lends some exactness of thought and some terseness of expression to practical minds. But Ruskin is only one of the notable instances which go far to prove that the greatest writers of the century—Keats, Walter Scott, Carlyle, Browning—were men who hardly came under classical influences at all; while other great writers—Wordsworth, Tennyson, Byron, and Shelley—obtained no distinction in academical exercises; and the few great writers whom our universities rewarded, such as Matthew Arnold, Newman and Pater, can hardly be ranked among the leading literary influences of the century."

Mr. Benson's charge, in this long passage, that a classical education places imitation before self-expression, and conformity to rule before originality, is one that can fairly be made of any century; preëminently, in England, of the eighteenth. But the nineteenth was romantic and reacted against the principles Mr. Benson deplores. Even a romantic century, however, is powerless to remain uninfluenced by the Classics. Such a century catches the spirit of the past, or tries to. To say that Keats, Scott, Carlyle and Browning were men who hardly came under classical influences at all is hardly a true statement of the facts; and if Wordsworth, Tennyson, Byron and Shelley won no distinction in academical exercises, they were influenced by the Classics, nevertheless, in very marked though very different manners. For that matter the most classical of the century's writers, Landor, won no academic distinction either. As for Arnold, Newman and Pater, one, at least, namely Arnold, *can* be ranked among the leading literary influences of the century.

In another vein than Mr. Benson's mis-statements and half-truths are the opening words of E. Vernon Arnold's *Roman Stoicism*. "In the generations preceding our own," says he, "classical study has, to a large extent, attended to form rather than matter, to expression rather than content. To-day it is beginning to take a wider outlook. We are learning to look on literature as an unveiling of the human mind in its various stages of development, and as a key to the true meaning of history."

The Classical Influence in English Literature

One of the pleasant features of an examination of the classical influence in the nineteenth century lies in noting the appearance among Englishmen of letters (before its appearance among English scholars) of an impatience of the letter and a yearning for the spirit and content of ancient literature and life.

More specifically, De Quincey advocated translations as a means for getting at Greek thought; Landor did a great amount of reading of Latin and Greek after his expulsion from the University and passed independent judgment on it; William Allingham was advised by Landor to learn Greek grammar, as being more comprehensive, before Latin, and by Clough to regard Latin as living, a sort of ante-Dantean Italian; Carlyle declared he had to acquire classical metres after he left school[15]; Ruskin disclaimed scholarship,[16] but knew much Latin and Greek; Macaulay read Classics for the pleasure they afforded him as literature,—in which he has been followed by the Trevelyans,—G. M. Trevelyan going so far as to make fun of the rigidity of English school classics-teaching in his *Poor Muggleton and the Classics;* Hartley Coleridge defended the study of minor classical writers, since he did not agree that they endangered the Latin style of modern school boys; Sydney Smith despised gerund-grinding; Thackeray mourned the mechanical teaching of Greek; Dickens satirized the theory that Greek and Latin should be forced arbitrarily upon all types of boys; George Eliot laughed at pedants and Englishmen who studied Classics as the proper pursuits of gentlemen; and Trollope, dissatisfied with his school training in Latin, learned to appreciate Latin literature only in later life.[17]

[15] Froude, "Life," I.　　　[16] "Praeterita," I, ch. XI, § 220.
[17] "Autobiography," ch. VI.

The Classical Influence in English Literature

In the *Atlantic Monthly* for July, 1914, Mr. John Jay Chapman writes of *The Greek Genius.*

"The Greek Genius," says he, "is so different from the modern English genius that they cannot understand one another. How shall we come to see this clearly? The matter is difficult in the extreme; because we are all soaked in modern feeling, and in America we are all drenched in British influence. The desire of Britain to annex ancient Greece, the deep-felt need that the British writers and poets of the nineteenth century have shown to edge and nudge nearer to Greek feeling, is familiar to all of us. Swinburne expresses his Hellenic longings by his hymeneal strains, Matthew Arnold by sweetness and light, Gilbert Murray by sweetness and pathos,—and all through the divine right of Victorian expansion. It has been a profoundly unconscious development in all these men. They have instinctively and innocently attached their little oil-can to the coat-tails of Euripides and of the other great Attic writers. They have not been interested in Greek for its own sake. They have been interested in the exploitation of Greece for the purpose of British consumption."

"The divine right of Victorian expansion" is a good phrase, and one to keep. But to call this expansion a "profoundly unconscious development" when applied to the Greek spirit by Swinburne, Arnold and Murray, and to add that instinct and naïveté rather than interest in Greek for its own sake was the motive power behind them is uncritical, to say the least.

In *Apollo Indicted* (*Forum*, July, 1915) Mr. Will Hutchins has written a eulogy of Euripides as a playwright and of Gilbert Murray as his translator. But in his opening paragraph he follows Mr. Chapman — to whom he refers — in making further rash statements regarding the Greek spirit. He says we may "fairly question the authenticity of what may be called the Greek strain in English poetry;" and supports his position by pointing to *Samson Agonistes* and *Atalanta in Calydon*. Both of these poetical dramas, says he, we are told have captured the Greek spirit; yet the one is really Biblical, the other rapturously modern. If the Greek spirit is capable of informing both the sober Milton and the intoxicated Swinburne, then what sort of an adventuress, asks he, is the Greek Muse, anyway? Are not Old Testament Puritanism and modern paganism mutually exclusive, and is not the Greek spirit, if it is said to be in both, a spirit indeed; nay a phantom like the Trojan Helen of Stesichorus?

I believe it is not. For my conception of the Greek spirit is broader than Mr. Hutchins', who evidently limits his to "restraint, essential and emotional impulse, and inclusive breadth." To me the Greek spirit is the spirit of Greek literature entire,— the Greek genius, in short; and that is not a very narrow, but a very broad thing, not a wraith nor an abstraction, but the living, growing and changing forms of the Greek arts. In it are included not only classical but romantic and realistic elements,— all the strains that enter into Greek literature, living or "dead:" all, finally, that Mr. Livingstone includes in his *The Greek Genius and Its Meaning to Us,*— namely, the notes of Beauty, Freedom, Directness, Humanism, Sanity and Manysidedness,— and all that he rejects in his Introduction. "For in fact," he admits on page 16 of the latter, "the Greeks were parents alike of ribaldry and of high moral endeavour, of rationalism and of emotional worship, of Socrates and of Pythagoras, of Aristophanes and of Zeno. They are the epitome of human nature. *Quemvis hominum secum attulit ad nos:* the Greek has brought us all humanity wrapped up in himself, and any one who attempts a book on his genius will learn in the writing to beware of denying him any quality."

Mr. Hutchins makes merry over the British poets' wooing of the antique Muse, "like the gentlemen they were, toiling abroad for her like Jacob for Rachel." To him the Greek spirit is something fixed, final and defined, governed by rules, to be approached, besought and won in an orderly, conventional manner. Perhaps French poets have so wooed; the English have not.

The Englishman — especially the nineteenth century Englishman — finds the Greek genius so complex that he can discover Puritanism, paganism, temperance, extravagance, tragedy, comedy, didacticism, emotionalism, classicism, romanticism or realism in it as he pleases. Landor is attracted by Epicurus, Greek lyric and elegy; Southey by Epictetus; Macaulay by Greek history and oratory; Lamb by Hesiod; Moore by Anacreon; Keats by Homer; Shelley by Plato; Peacock by Aristophanes, Lucian and Nonnus; Meredith by Menander; Rossetti by Sappho; Wilde by the Anthology; Swinburne by Sappho, Catullus, Pindar and Aeschylus; Jefferies by Diogenes Laertius; FitzGerald by Plato; Kingsley by the Alexandrians; Arnold by Homer and Empedocles; Tennyson by Virgil; Browning by Euripides and Aristophanes; Mrs. Browning by Aeschylus and Sappho; Andrew Lang by Homer and Theocritus; Thomas Hardy by Sophocles, and Robert Bridges by Aeschylus and Menander.

I confess that if Mr. Hutchins had questioned the Greek strain in the English prose of the century rather than in its English poetry my task would be simpler. I should then show how FitzGerald put Plato into *Euphranor;* how Peacock put Lucian and Aristophanes into his novels; how Macaulay composed *Scenes from Athenian Revels* and kept Demosthenes and Thucydides before him in his speeches and histories; how Kingsley put the Alexandrian world, pagan and Christian into *Hypatia;* how Newman put some of it into *Callista;* how Landor made Greece live in *Pericles and Aspasia* and in certain of his *Imaginary Conversations;* how Carlyle chanted his *French Revolution* in strains Homeric and Greek-tragic; how Bulwer-Lytton did his part in *Pausanias the Spartan* and Mrs. Lynn Linton in *Amymone, a Romance of the Days of Pericles;* how even Thackeray caught the Greek spirit when he visited Greece and saw the Parthenon; how Jefferies wove his conception of Greek beauty into *Amaryllis at the Fair;* how Wilde made charming Greek sketches in his *Intentions;* how Traill was influenced by Lucian to write a *New Lucian* and Mallock by Plato to compose a *New Republic*.

Or if I wrote of translations and paraphrases — Sotheby's, Mitchell's, Hunt's, Campbell's, Milman's, Byron's, the Brownings', Morris's, FitzGerald's, Calverley's, Frere's, Rogers', Blackie's, Jowett's and Lang's — to say nothing of the dry but useful Bohns — these might help in establishing the "strain." Or if I pointed to mythology in prose — to Lamb's, Landor's, Carlyle's, Ruskin's, Disraeli's, Meredith's and Stevenson's — these would go far to establish Greek atmosphere, especially in the cases of Ruskin and Meredith. Or if I showed the Greek influence coming through the Latin—but I reserve that, for a moment.

Instead of all these kindred manifestations I return to the Greek note in nineteenth century poetry. Here we find the classical Landor and the romantic Swinburne both drawing deep draughts from the spring, the one in the classical *Hellenics*, the other in the romantic *Atalanta* and the

Alexandrian *Ballads and Lyrics*. Here are Wilde, another Alexandrian; and Tennyson, a modern, following his usual method of treating ancient story in a novel fashion. Back of them loom Shelley and Keats, the one a mystic Platonist, the other an Alexandrian and a mediaevalist intoxicated with Greek mythology. The Greek strain is in all these men, though all make romantic use of it: even Landor does, at times. Two of them are restrained,— Landor and Tennyson — the others are fired by a romantic consuming flame, which they feed, with much intemperance, with Greek poetry. Nor are they all; for who would part with Browning's *tour de force* in realism, *Aristophanes Apology*, or with Mrs. Browning's *Wine of Cypress*, or with Morris's mediaeval rendering of the ancient spirit in *The Life and Death of Jason* and *The Earthly Paradise?* And among minors who shall despise Beddoes, Sir Lewis Morris, Grant Allen, Coventry Patmore, Aubrey de Vere, Lionel Johnson, Edwin Arnold, John Davidson, Andrew Lang, Alfred Austin, John Todhunter, William Watson, Robert Bridges, Lord De Tabley, Frederick Tennyson, Charles Tennyson Turner, Horace Smith, Robert Eyres Landor, Thomas Hood, Baron Thurlow, Reginald Heber, Henry Hart Milman, Thomas Noon Talfourd, John Hamilton Reynolds, Richard Henry Horne, John Stuart Blackie, Thomas Gordan Hake, Francis Hastings Doyle, William James Linton, Sir Joseph Noel Paton, Dora Greenwell, Thomas Woolner, Thomas Westwood, Mortimer Collins, William Watson, Richard Watson Dixon, John Nichol, Richard Garnett, Thomas Ashe, David Gray, Mrs. Ernest Radford and Edward Dowden? None of these minors is negligible; all were persons and poets of taste. Most of them were romanticists not uninfluenced by the classical. Other poets, like Owen Meredith in *Marah*, and T. E.

Brown in *Israel and Hellas*, balance the claims of Hebraism and Hellenism, as Southey,[18] De Quincey,[19] Ruskin,[20] Carlyle[21] and Arnold[22] do in prose or life. And Francis Thompson, in an essay on *Paganism Old and New* declares only paganism with a Christian leaven in it is true paganism. Finally Ruskin and Pater are forever pointing out the moral and the ascetic strains in the Greek character.[23]

And with all this said, a further triumph of nineteenth century art remains in its use of mythology. Wordsworth tried to dispense with it and gave up the attempt.[24] Byron played with it; Shelley soared with it; Swinburne and Wilde revelled in it; Tennyson and Sir Lewis Morris modernized it; Mrs. Browning loved it; Browning acknowledged it and Beddoes gave his sombre imaginative touch to it. In a word, majors and minors put it to their several uses, conscious how mythology can be abused if over-used: used it as current poetical coin, as humor, as cloud imagery, as metaphor, as ancient, mediaeval and modern coloring.[25]

I turn from the Greek influence to the Roman. "The literature of Greece proper does not cease to attract us by its originality, charm and variety," says Arnold in his *Roman Stoicism*, p. 1; "but the new interest may yet find its fullest satisfaction in Roman literature: for of all ancient peoples the Romans achieved most, and their achieve-

---

[18] i. e. he was influenced alike by the Bible and Epictetus.
[19] "Letters to a Young Man," III.
[20] "Memorial Studies of St. Mark's."
[21] Note the mingling of the two in the style of "The French Revolution."
[22] "Hebraism and Hellenism."
[23] See Ruskin's "The Queen of the Air," I, "Athena Chalinitis," 49; "Modern Painters," Pt. IX, ch. II, "The Lance of Pallas," 14; and Pater's "Plato and Platonism."
[24] Preface to his "Ode to Lycoris."
[25] For the mythology of the century see Gayley's "Classic Myths in English Literature," and Edward C. Guild's "A List of Poems Illustrating Greek Myth in the English Poetry of the Nineteenth Century." (Bowdoin College Library Bulletin, No. 1, 1891.)

ments have been the most enduring." There is a large *perhaps* about the statement, but this much is true — Rome not only gave of herself largely to the modern world, but absorbed and passed on much of Greece. And if the romantic nineteenth century found greater affinity for its romanticism in Greece than in Rome, it did not neglect Rome.

The use of Latin quotations in Parliament,[26] in novels and in Thomas Moore's footnotes need not detain us; nor the influence of Cicero on the styles of De Quincey, Macaulay, Newman and Stevenson; nor that of Latin generally on the language of Thomas Hardy. In contrast to the latter's over-Latinized manner is Landor's carefully chosen style, with its criticism and rejection of Milton's Latinisms. Nor do we need to point out again Thackeray's, Bulwer-Lytton's and Dowson's love of Horace, Byron's good-natured use of him, and Meredith's impatience of his philosophy; Hartley Coleridge's[27] and Morris's[28] affection for Pliny; Peacock's[29] and Pater's[30] for Apuleius; Macaulay's for Cicero and Catullus; Wordsworth's, Ruskin's and Tennyson's for Virgil; the Epicurean FitzGerald's[31] for the Stoic Seneca; Beddoes' for Seneca the tragedian; Rossetti's for *Gesta Romanorum* and St. Augustine; and Mrs. Browning's and Lionel Johnson's for Lucretius.

Instead, we note especially the interest the century felt in viewing Rome archaeologically, with Wordsworth,

---

[26] See Herbert Paul: "The Decay of Classical Quotation," in his "Men and Letters."
[27] "Memoirs of Roger Ascham."
[28] May Morris, Introduction to vol. XXII of Morris's Works.
[29] "Gryll Grange," ch. IV.   [30] "Marius the Epicurean."
[31] Wright: "Letters and Literary Remains of Edward Fitzgerald," 1889, I, 124, 144, 311.

The Classical Influence in English Literature

Scott and Hardy, and in visiting and living in Italy[32] and singing Italian liberty,[33] with Shelley, Keats, Byron, Landor, Ruskin, the Brownings, the Rossettis, Meredith, Swinburne, Dickens, George Eliot, Bulwer-Lytton, Owen Meredith, Wilkie Collins, William Sharp, Samuel Rogers, Arthur Hugh Clough, Barry Cornwall, Sydney Dobell, Lord Houghton, Richard Jefferies, John Addington Symonds, T. E. Brown, Robert Buchanan, Aubrey de Vere, Samuel Butler, Alfred Austin, Macaulay, the Trevelyans, Cary, William Trevenix French, Alfred Domett, William James Linton, John Nichol, Herman Charles Merivale, David Gray, Mrs. Hamilton King and Madame Darmesteter. Nor should we neglect the partly classical, partly romantic influence of France on the Brontës, Arnold, Meredith, Swinburne, Stevenson, Moore, Dowson, Henley, Lang, Symons, Dobson and Gosse.

Again, while Hellenism and Hebraism contended in the works of Ruskin and Arnold, while Landor criticized Plato and praised Epicurus and Aristotle,[34] and while Shelley and Pater embraced Plato, Roman philosophy was not quite forgotten, with Macaulay interested in Cicero's eclecticism, FitzGerald in Seneca's Stoicism, and Mrs. Browning, Tennyson, Lionel Johnson and Mallock in Lucretius's Epicureanism.

There remain poems and prose tales that capture or aim to capture the spirit of ancient Rome. These are Landor's *Imaginary Conversations, Roman,* Pater's *Marius the Epicurean,* Bulwer-Lytton's *Last Days of Pompeii,*

---

[32] For a partial account, see A. G. S. Canning's "British Writers on Classic Lands," 1907.

[33] For a selection, see G. M. Trevelyan's "English Songs of Italian Freedom," 1911, with its valuable introduction and notes.

[34] Wm. Chislett, Jr.: "Walter Savage Landor and His Relation to the Classical Tradition in English Literature," (Master's Thesis, Stanford University, 1912.)

The Classical Influence in English Literature

Atherstone's *Last Days of Herculaneum,* Collins' *Antonina, or the Fall of Rome,* Byron's *Childe Harold,* Rogers' *Italy,* Macaulay's *Lays of Ancient Rome* and *Fragment of a Roman Tale,* Barry Cornwall's *Julian the Apostate,* Trevelyan's breezy *Horace at the University of Athens,* Bridges' *History of Nero,* Robert Landor's *Fountain of Arethusa,* Doyle's *Gythia,* Nichol's *Hannibal,* and Reade's *Catiline* and *Italy.*

We have surveyed the nineteenth century by authors, summarized them and dealt with them under the different phases of the classical influence. What is our conclusion? That Greece and Rome did not die in the romantic, realistic nineteenth century nor are likely to in the unfathomed twentieth. Through philology, archaeology, interest in ancient philosophy, admiration for the graceful Greek tongue and the mosaic-like architectonic Latin, a use and not abuse of mythology, a very wide reading of ancient authors, major and minor, in the original and in translations, and finally through the vivifying of ancient life by travel and by prose and poetry embodying the ancient spirit, Greece and Rome have lived as never before, and bid fair to live while men and arts endure.

PART II

Other Essays and Notes

I
The Platonic Love of Walter Pater

IN *Winckelmann* Pater quotes the great Hellenist as saying: "I have noticed that those who are observant of beauty only in women, and are moved little or not at all by the beauty of men, seldom have an impartial, vital, inborn instinct for beauty in art. To such persons the beauty of Greek art will ever seem wanting, because its supreme beauty is rather male than female." Yet Walter Savage Landor, the master of classicism in English, was more moved by the beauty of women than of men. Indeed, this partiality for the Sex puts Sydney Colvin ill at ease, for a moment, in Landor's Garden of Epicurus. "His young women," says the critic in his Life of Landor, *"including the Greek,* are apt to comport themselves in a manner giggly, missish and disconcerting." Yet H. W. Boynton in the *Atlantic* and Melville Best Anderson in the *Dial* find these nymphlike creatures charming; while Brandes in *Main Currents in Nineteenth Century Literature* says finely that Landor was the discoverer of Greek girlhood.

Pater's classicism, then, owes much to men, Landor's more to women. Yet Pater aimed not to do things by halves. He was a student of Culture, a lover of Beauty, in three clearly marked periods. Phases of antiquity, the Renaissance and modern Europe live in his magic style. He could not, then, conceivably ignore women entirely. What was his attitude towards "one-half the human race?"

That he did not forget women utterly is at once recalled by his famous interpretation of the *Mona Lisa*. Antiquity and all succeeding ages live in her, "the deposit, little cell by cell, of strange thoughts and fantastic reveries and exquisite passions." She is "the embodiment of the old fancy, the symbol of the modern idea." Yet "set her for a moment beside one of those white Greek goddesses or beautiful women of antiquity, and how would they be troubled by this beauty, into which the soul with all its maladies has passed?" Rather is she comparable to Demeter in *Greek Studies*, "the weary woman, our Lady of Sorrows, the *mater dolorosa* of the ancient world."

What then moved Pater, we ask; since he was moved in a measure, by fair feminine personalities, at least in books and art? Spiritual beauty, or physical and intellectual beauty as well? And how did he react to outward charm in women,—as something disquieting to his "sense of sexual wholeness," or radiant, glorious and inspiring, as to Whitman and Meredith?

The latter's "women of beauty and brains" he understood hardly at all, to judge from a passage in the *Essay on Style* (1888). "The artist," says he, "is of necessity a scholar, and in what he proposes to do will have in mind, first of all, the scholar and the scholarly conscience—the male conscience in this matter, as we must think it, under a system of education which still to so large an extent limits real scholarship to men."

But if he has little experience and appreciation of intellectual women (yet see his review of *Robert Elsmere;* a literary letter to Mrs. Ward quoted by his biographer Benson; another from Lady Dilke concerning him and his friendship for Miss Robinson, the novelist) he has more to say of women's spiritual nature. In *Diaphaneité*, after naming some unworldly types that the world is yet able to estimate, he says, "There is another type of character which is not broad and general, rare, precious above all to the artist, a character which seems to have been the supreme moral charm in the Beatrice of the Commedia. It does not take the eye by breadth of colour; rather it is that fine edge of light, where the elements of our moral nature refine themselves to the burning point." Again, Leonardo's women "are the clairvoyants through whom, as through delicate instruments, one becomes aware of the subtler forces of nature." At Heidelberg, too, where Pater spent his vacations with his sisters and aunt, he composed *St. Gertrude of Himmelstadt,* a story in prose. The heroine breathes courage into the fainting soldiers who defend her castle. "Thus," says Thomas Wright, drawing the moral, as often, in his *Life of Pater,* "thus to man contending in life's battle, but 'weary and wounded and sorely pressed' woman hath ever help."

When we ask if Pater was correspondingly moved by the physical beauty of women we recall the words of W. Ayott Orton, in the *Westminster Review,* November, 1908. "Everything," says he, "even the most recondite of abstractions, seemed to possess for him a sort of quasi-sensuous appeal." In Mallock's amusing caricature of Pater in the *New Republic,* Mr. Rose is made out exceedingly sensitive to all beauty, including woman's. Again, if we are to believe Mr. Wright, Pater wrote as a boy *Cassandra,* a mournful and slightly sensual poem "to which McQueen objected, but which Pater refused to change."

The *Fan of Fire,* however, was a religious effusion. Pater is disclosed on a hill-top with a lady. "Turning to her," says his playful biographer, "and taking her hand he declares he is overpowered,—by the scene. . . . . He loves the earth, he says, her trees, her very stones." In another poem St. Elizabeth of Hungary is celebrated in a spirit of extreme asceticism. "The saint is represented," says Wright "as fixing her thoughts on Heaven and as living, though married, in a state of virginity."

But Pater in vacation, in Mr. Mallock's satire and in youth is not the Pater of *Marius, Gaston de Latour* and the *Imaginary Portraits*. The true Pater is the disciple of Winckelmann (and of Plato, as we shall show); one who, says Mr. Benson, "could devote himself to the passionate contemplation of beauty, without any taint or grossness of sense, who was penetrated by fiery emotion, but without any dalliance in feminine sentiment, whose sensitiveness was preternaturally acute, while his conception was cool and firm." A case in point is Pater's eulogy of Rossetti, that superb painter of the physical charm of women. Mr. Benson says of the essay: "One cannot help feeling that the innermost world of mystical passion in which Rossetti lived was as a locked and darkened chamber to Pater..... To be intellectually and perceptively impassioned, indeed, he desired; but the physical ardours of love, the longing for enamoured possession,—with this Pater had nothing in common."

"Upon my appealing to Pater once," says Frederick Wedmore, in *Memories*, "to be moved by some singular exhibition of womanly beauty, more probably in Art than in Life, he responded, I remember, but coldly, though he sought for an explanation, or had it at hand. His life at Oxford, he said, had made him so much more familiar with the beauty of boyhood, the beauty of male youth. One must have known Pater better than I did, to know whether, at all — in days remote or recent — he had ever had a love affair." Pater is noted for his intellectual and spiritual biographies of men. For these he drew upon his own mental life, that of his men friends and the college students among whom he lived. In addition there were always books to supplement life. But when he wrote of women he was ill at ease; for then he became nearly dependent on books and pictures. He knew the sentimental *Paul and Virginia* by heart, he was enthusiastic over Browning's *Men and Women* and he was fond of French novels. He planned to write on the impassioned verse of Sappho, but his intention never materialized. Marius does not fall in love, and his life affords only glimpses of his mother, the Empress Faustina and the Christian widow Cecilia. Gaston de Latour marries, but before Colombe reaches human size the story is abandoned, and remains a striking fragment. Sebastian and Emerald Uthwart, Denys and Apollyon give no thought to the other sex. Pater himself admired *Romola* not for the complex soul of its heroine, but for the figure of Savanarola and the Renaissance coloring. The passage in the book that best pleased him, says Wright, was, "The most passionate life is in form and colour."

Critics have deprived Pater of even a trace of originality in his creation of Colombe and in his interpretations of the *Mona Lisa*. Wright holds that Gaston and Colombe are merely Abelard and Heloise altered to taste. T. P. Armstrong, in the *Saturday Review*,[*] points out that there were already strictures on the character of Mona Lisa in George Sand, Theophile Gautier and Michelet. "It is certainly more likely," says the writer, "that any 'story' that may have arisen with regard to the Joconde should have originated in the 'Ville Lumière,' where the picture was constantly on view, than in the brain of an Oxford don, whose ingenuity, however, I do not wish to depreciate."

[*] Jan. 3, 1914.

Other Essays and Notes

J. M. Kennedy[1] is uncritical when he says, "It would be possible to say a good deal more about Pater from a critical standpoint if we had more particulars about his sexual feelings." Lewis Greenslet[2] speaks the last word on that subject when he writes, "So he came, one thinks, like the object of one of his own characterizations, to a kind of moral sexlessness, a kind of impotence, an ineffectual wholeness of nature, yet with a true beauty and significance of its own."

To quibble a moment: Edward FitzGerald was fond of reiterating, "Taste is the feminine of genius." Now Pater had genius — a masculine virtue always to him — and he had taste, a feminine quality to FitzGerald. Therefore in himself he combined the masculine and the feminine. But sophistry or truth, as we like, Pater's wholeness of nature circumscribed his activity as an artist.

Pater's interest in women, then, was confined to a mild intellectual appreciation of their spiritual, intellectual and physical qualities and charms. Yet Edward Dowden concludes an essay on Pater with the statement that "Pater is before all else a lover. Infinite patience," he adds, "quite as much as fire, is the mood of all true lovers."

Pater was a lover, but a Platonic lover, and he did not love women, even platonically. He loved Philosophy, Greek that he was, and he attained it Platonically, by passing lingeringly from delightful association with fair outward objects to the Platonic realms of perfect ideas. Nothing ignoble marked his ascent. He lived the life of a writer, a teacher, and a friend of boys. Through Platonic enthusiasm he idealized an existence dull and drab to persons who dislike teaching, and ascended into the Platonists' spheres of the Ideal and the Beautiful.

[1] "English Literature, 1880-1905," 1913.   [2] "Walter Pater."

Other Essays and Notes

In *the Poetry of Michelangelo,* however, he shows how Platonism may be attained by love of women, the normal medium for mediæval and modern Neoplatonists. "It is the Platonic tradition rather than Dante's that has moulded Michelangelo's verse," says he. "In many ways no sentiment could have been less like Dante's love for Beatrice than Michelangelo's for Vittoria Colonna.... Michelangelo is always passing forward from the outward beauty—*il bel del fuor che agli occhi piace* — to apprehend the unseen beauty; *trascenda nella forma universale* — that abstract form of beauty, about which Platonists reason."

But Pater, like Winckelmann, apprehended Hellenism in Greek, not in modern fashion. Of Winckelmann, Pater says, "That his affinity with Hellenism was not merely intellectual, that the subtler threads of temperament were inwoven in it, is proved by his romantic, fervent friendship with young men." As for Pater's own Platonism, that is best seen and recorded in his lectures on *Plato and Platonism.* He unfolds, before his students, the Greek Academe. He does not devote a lecture to Platonic love, but he mentions it in chapters on *Lacedaemon, The Doctrine of Plato* and *The Genius of Plato* (q. v.). Macaulay and Landor accuse the *Phaedrus* and *Symposium* of immorality; if Pater believes them anything but moral, he does not say so. Perhaps he rather sees the good in Platonic love,—comradeship and affection between men—and ignores the evil; as in *The Renaissance* and in *Marius* he is concerned with the virtues and not the vices of Epicureanism. Throughout his work Pater has only respect for the senses and their constant refinement; he has no interest in or sympathy with sensuality. In Plato's doctrine he sees a most spiritual philosophy evolved through the senses, chiefly through the eye. He shuts his own to the ugly in the system, if he sees it at all. His Platonic love is gracious and refined, a pure affection for healthy male youth and beautiful Ideas.

"Pater was condemned by temperament to a certain isolation," says Benson; "he was outside the world, and not of it. A happy marriage might have brought him more into line with humanity."

Pater did not marry. He wedded himself, rather, to Beauty, Art, Literature and Philosophy. His offspring were his magical writings. But they have suffered, as have many of Swinburne's. Where is the sane strength of Meredith or Arnold in either? They want even the warm humanity of Tennyson, whose sentiment was saved from sentimentality (Meredith notwithstanding) by hearth and home, so that Englishmen followed him and proclaimed him first poet of the age.

As Americans, we are irresistibly moved to speculate on Pater's probable development had he taught young men and women in a co-educational college instead of young men only at Oxford. A parallel instance is at hand. Trained at Harvard, William Vaughn Moody returned to his native Middle West to teach mixed classes at Chicago. His letters disclose his reaction. He taught women; he was repelled and attracted by turns; he proposed to one Western girl who sent him elegiac on his way. He profited from his experience. He grew steadily in understanding of women. He studied Art, literature, men and women. Barring occasional bad taste, in fact, his women are nearly as powerfully conceived as any in English letters. Pater drew no real women; and his men are more one-sided than Moody's women; all mind and spirit.

The New World, coupled with the Old, made a great poet of Moody. The Old World, rich with culture, unshaken for him, by the disquieting spirit of the new, made a marvelous prose stylist of Walter Pater. Both were mystics, both were aesthetes, both sipped the exquisite from Art. But one painted life from men, women and books; the other wove a gorgeous tapestry from his inner life, books, boys and pictures.

II

The New Hellenism of Oscar Wilde

In Act II of Wilde's *A Woman of No Importance* the following dialogue occurs:—

> *Mrs. Allonby:* The American girl has been giving us a lecture.
> *Lord Illingworth:* Really? All Americans lecture, I believe. I suppose it is something in their climate. What did she lecture about?
> *Mrs. Allonby:* Oh, Puritanism, of course.

Eventually, however, the young Puritan accepts the woman of no importance as her mother-in-law.

In this essay we shall give Wilde an American lecture on his false Hellenism; but accept him, in part, in spite of his theory. "The fact of a man's being a poisoner is nothing against his style," says Wilde in *Pen, Pencil, and Poison*. The fact of Wilde's being Hellenistic is not everything against his Hellenism, but it is something.

Moreover, Wilde lectured himself. When he was in condition he defended Art for Art's Sake, the New Hellenism, and the New Individualism with all the conviction of England's chief advocate of those tenets. When he was discouraged, or recovering from excesses, or languishing in prison, or when the true artist in him suddenly saw the false, he cried out against himself and his theories with a fervor like unto Bunyan's in *Grace Abounding*.

Wilde's poetry is his record of disillusion. Once he mourns (in *Humanitad*):—

> But we are Learning's changelings, know by rote
> The clarion watchword of each Grecian school
> And follow none, the flawless sword that smote
> The pagan Hydra is an effete tool
> Which we ourselves have blunted, what man now
> Shall scale the august ancient heights and to old
> Reverence bow?

Not Wilde, surely, as he confesses in the same poem:—

> And yet I cannot tread the portico
> And live without desire, fear, and pain,
> Or nurture that wise calm which long ago
> The grave Athenian master taught to men,
> Self-poised, self-centred, and self-comforted,
> To watch the world's vain phantasies go by
> with unbowed head.

Rather he yielded himself to the full flood of unrestraint and let himself drift on the uncharted seas, that wind and sun and storm might blow and warm and wrack him and leave their mark upon him:—

> For he who lives more lives than one
> More deaths than one must die,—

he sings in *The Ballad of Reading Gaol*. In *Helas!*, his prologue to the *Poems* of 1881, he wavers momentarily:—

> To drift with every passion till my soul
> Is a stringed lute on which all winds can play,
> Is it for this that I have given away
> Mine ancient wisdom and austere control?

But at once he is off again on his mad quest of Beauty, Liberty, Life, and Pleasure. "I amused myself," he says in *De Profundis*, "with being a *flâneur*, a dandy, a man of fashion. I surrounded myself with the smaller natures and the meaner minds. I became the spendthrift of my own genius, and to waste an eternal youth gave me a certain joy.

Tired of being on the heights, I deliberately went to the depths."

In *The Picture of Dorian Gray* Lord Henry declares that if one man were to realize himself completely the world would so gain in joy as to blot out mediævalism and attain to the Hellenic ideal,—"to something finer, richer, than the Hellenic ideal, it may be." This advance over Hellenism, even, Wilde calls the New Hellenism. He uses the term in *The Soul of Man Under Socialism,* but sets forth his conception more clearly in *L'Envoi* and in *The English Renaissance.* In the former he points out that Ruskin's æsthetic system is ethical always; whereas "we who are no longer with him" have passed on into that "serene House" where "the rule of art is the rule of beauty,"—wherein dwells "the gladness that comes, not from the rejection, but the absorption, of all passion." In *The English Renaissance* he defines his New Hellenism still more specifically, by synthesizing those hard-won analytical terms, Classical and Romantic. "It is really from the union of Hellenism," says he, "in its breadth, its sanity of purpose, its calm possession of beauty, with the adventitive, the intensified individualism, the passionate colour of the romantic spirit, that springs the art of the nineteenth century in England, as from the marriage of Faust and Helen of Troy sprang the beautiful boy Euphorion." Now no better characterization of nineteenth-century eclecticism exists than that. But Wilde at once qualifies. Instead of including the elements of strength and poise that normally accompany classicism, he rejects them for the sole ideals of Art and Beauty. All else he demolishes, in the name of Liberty, with paradox. "The way of paradoxes," he says elsewhere, "is the way of truth. To test Reality we must see it on the tight-rope. When the Verities become acrobats we can judge them."

Out of the agony and humility of the *De Profundis,* it is only just to add, emerges a new self leading the old: his New Individualism, his New Hellenism in the leash of a truer Individualism, of a calmer Hellenism,—for we are not of those who doubt Wilde's suffering, or his repentance: yet all of him remains at the service of Art for Art's Sake. This, his most cherished theory, goes with him to the grave. He declares himself more of an individualist than ever. "Christ is the most supreme of individualists," he adds. He expresses a wish to write of Christ as the precursor of the romantic movement in life and of the artistic life considered in its relation to conduct. Then he praises the Greeks because they never chattered about sunsets; only to cry out at the end for the Mystical in Art, the Mystical in Life; a chastened Pagan reaching out for the Soul in Things.

"The Germans," according to Nicoll and Seccombe in their *History of English Literature,* "have taken Wilde's Art for Art theories seriously and have produced and criticized his *Salomé* and other paradoxically intense but insincere æsthetic products with amazing gravity." Our American Puritanism might conceivably show with equal gravity that Wilde's Art for Art theories were sufficiently weak morally to lead in themselves to his downfall. Wilde anticipated such a possibility. "People point to *Reading Gaol,*" says he in *De Profundis,* "and say, 'That is where the artistic life leads a man.' Well," answers our irrepressible individualist, caught, as he says he is, for forgetting his Individualism and for calling on society to punish the Marquis of Queensbury for libeling *him,* "it might lead to worse places"; whereupon he shows that sorrow will make him a greater artist than before.

Other Essays and Notes

Since the world has condemned his morals, since the Germans have discussed his Art for Art's Sake, and since Wilde has anticipated and partly answered the question of the artistic life in its relation to conduct, we content ourselves here with pointing out how well equipped he was in the Classics, especially in Greek; and how little they really influenced his Art, except as they substantiated his own theories and satisfied his cravings for Romanticism. All else in the Classic temper was perfect to him, but unattainable.

Wilde's college record in Classics was of the highest. He was an "A" student. He read Classics with all the facility of a paragon. So easy were Latin and Greek authors to him that he seldom paused to ask just what they meant. He was far too glib for that. Besides, he had theories of what they should mean. His *The Rise of Historical Criticism* illustrates both points. He wrote the paper in competition for the Chancellor's English Essay at Oxford, in 1879. It is an uninspired piece of work, dry and formal, indeed, and was not accepted. "Historical criticism," says he, in an original moment, "is a part of that complex working towards freedom which may be described as the revolt against authority." He finds this tendency entirely Greek. He declares the Roman respect for tradition "fatal to any rise of that spirit of revolt against authority, the importance of which, as a factor in intellectual progress, we have already seen." His highest commendation is reserved for Polybius, the historian of Roman institutions, whom he praises for his rationalistic method. Herodotus and Thucydides are treated at some length; Plutarch, Livy, Sallust, and Tacitus are touched upon. Plato and Aristotle are considered conventionally. Homer, Hesiod, Pindar, Corinna, Heraclitus, Æschylus, Euripides, Xenophon, Zeno,

Other Essays and Notes

Epicurus, Euhemerus, Strabo, Ennius, Lucretius, Cicero, Minucius Felix and St. Augustine are mentioned.

The flower of Wilde's classical appreciation and art criticism is contained in his *Intentions*, a continuation and expansion, in part, of his *Rise of Historical Criticism*. With sufficient cigarettes and reassurances that the moon is not looking, he insinuates the names, at least, of Homer, Herodotus, Aristophanes, Sophocles, Euripides, Plato, Aristotle, Pausanias, Lucian, Livy, Pliny, Cicero, Virgil, Horace, Tacitus, Suetonius, and Fronto. All illustrate for him the antiquity of criticism; whence he advances to his own theory that the critic is an artist, inasmuch as he gazes on Art, then reacts and creates Art in describing Art. Whether the critic sees what the artist had in mind is of little moment; he sees something. Pater's interpretation of the *Mona Lisa* fulfills this ideal.

Indeed, much of Wilde's Art for Art's Sake came direct from Pater.[3] What he did not absorb from his master, however, was Pater's reverence for Plato,—that endless pilgrimage towards an understanding of the Greek spirit in the loftiest of the Greeks.[4] Wilde's heart goes out, rather, to Sappho, Theocritus, Catullus, Euripides, Aristophanes, Cicero's Letters, and the more picturesque portions of Homer and Suetonius. Of the Greek Anthology he says finely: "The beautiful poems contained in this collection seem to me to hold the same position in regard to the Greek dramatic literature as do the delicate little figurines of Tanagra to the Phidian marbles, to be quite as necessary for the com-

---

[3] For the relations of Pater and Wilde, see Dr. Edouard J. Bock's "Walter Pater's Einfluss Auf Oscar Wilde" (Bonn, 1913).

[4] Plato was too ethical for Wilde. When Socrates, for example, discusses art in the first book of the "Republic" he shows that Art for Art's Sake is Art for Conduct's sake and Art for the Object's sake. However, Wilde found portions of the "Symposium" and the "Phaedrus" more to his liking.

plete understanding of the Greek spirit.'' Truly they are, but in time these little things came to usurp for Wilde the places of the big things. In like manner, he was always on the point of realizing the full power of Dante and Shakespeare and never quite accomplishing his intentions. He got as far as the *Sonnets*.

The defects of Wilde's Hellenism are strikingly apparent in his Greek poems. Here Beauty and Liberty decline, at the worst, into Ugliness and Libertinage. Even structurally these poems stagger with intoxication. At the same time they flash forth illuminated lines and passages glowing with beauty and art.

But Homer E. Woodbridge in *Poet-Lore* has written so well of Wilde's poetry, *pro* and *con*, that we have nothing to add. Turning to his prose, and granting Wilde his *donnée* of a New Hellenism of Art and Beauty, we find him often artistic and often beautiful. If we cannot admit that his paradoxes, except in his inimitable comedies, are either artistic or beautiful, but feel that they are what many Philistines called them when Wilde was lecturing in America, namely, disgusting, we can dismiss them without loss. If along with them we cast out his passages of exaggerated romanticism, there remains, classically speaking, a body of real Art and Beauty. Critics who review all his prose are possessed of a desire to make a Selection from his writings. At its best his style is both artistic and beautiful in its nicety and flexibility. In his *English Poetesses* he looks for a new style, a new manner, from women. ''Their light touch and exquisite ear and delicate sense of balance and proportion would be no small service to us,'' he says. Such a manner, when he wrote best, was his own.

Wilde's fairy tales are so good that children read them and older people appreciate their wisdom and charm. There is hardly a discordant note in these finely graven stories. The opening description of his wildly romantic *Dorian Gray*, again, is perfect art. Only a Landor could equal his Homeric pictures in *The Critic as Artist*. His comedies, as Nicoll and Seccombe[5] say truly, exhibit the "quintessence of playful artifice, irresponsible persiflage and antiquarian wit skilfully modernized." Indeed, we can forgive Wilde his poor work for his comedies. In them he is no mean successor to Congreve and Sheridan. Even these illustrious predecessors did not outdo him in brilliant dialogue. He lacks the moral sincerity of Meredith's comedy and Molière's, but so do Congreve and Sheridan. In this one literary form, in short, his scorn of moral values does not disqualify him. Even ethically speaking, his comedies expose shams and discover good in persons generally considered bad. His tragedies, too, are interesting because they exhibit Wilde when he is not trying to be clever. *Vera, or the Nihilists*, though melodramatic is striking in conception. The *Florentine Tragedy* remains a fragment, finished but not begun! The *Duchess of Padua* is a good reading poetical drama.

Wilde, too, had the making of a critic. Had he, like Arnold, abandoned artistic production for criticism, he might have attained eminence. His characterizations of the styles of the Brownings, of Christina Rossetti, of Pater, and of Meredith show the keenest penetration and finest discrimination. His reviews range over such subjects as *Parnassus versus Philology, Modern Greek Poetry, To Read or Not to Read, Twelfth Night at Oxford, The Poetry of the People, Helena in Troas, Mr. Symonds' History of the Renaissance, A New Book on Dickens, Mr. Morris's Odyssey, Mr. Pater's Imaginary Conversations, Bowen's Virgil*

---

[5] "A History of English Literature," II, 780.

and *Aristotle at Afternoon Tea* (Mahaffy's *Art of Conversation*). His literary notes are innumerable. His *Miscellanies* contain essays on sculpture, bookbinding, dress, and other matters of art.

Wilde ruined his life for self-indulgence, for sensationlism and for theories. Unlike Pater and Whistler, he lacked the character to practice Art for Art's sake without harm to himself. Moreover, along with his life he spoiled much of his art. Indeed, that portion of his work that is sound was composed in defiance of or in spite of his theories. From this statement we have partially excepted his comedies, which reflect all sides of him in a glittering, dazzling shower of brilliant talk, the irresponsible, unscrupulous but amusing talk of his drawing-room, harmless as long as it is merely talk. But Wilde, in spite of his paradoxes, his self-consciousness, and his introspection, took his talk seriously. In prison he quotes his own epigrams.

Christ loves everyone but a Philistine, is the burden of his religious meditations in *De Profundis*. To Wilde Philistines are all persons who are moral and who oppose Art for Art's Sake. What Wilde will not admit, even from the depths, is that if artists are not born Philistines they should become so, at least morally. Hence he is to the end an extremist, a pseudo-Romanticist, a neo-Hellenist, a false Individualist. His New Hellenism was a passion, a disease, a poison. The Classics taught him to write a clear style. They failed to teach him measure, temperance, restraint. Classical calm was an ideal he could not attain, because he would not. He wrote clearly, but he did not see life clearly, nor see it whole.

III

The New Christianity of William Blake

THE New Hellenism of Oscar Wilde and The New Christianity of William Blake upheld freedom, impulse and unrestraint. Wilde's "the only way to get rid of temptation is to yield to it" might have been pronounced by Blake. Instead he wrote in *The Marriage of Heaven and Hell,* "The road of excess leads to the palace of wisdom."

Oscar Wilde, always an artist, went down through a decadent Hellenism, a diseased modernism, a budding futurism, drained the dregs of sense and rose again, in theory, through suffering and Christian forgiveness to higher ideals of art and conduct. William Blake rose up Neoplatonically, casting off Hellenism, the sway of the five senses, the rule of Reason, the human quest of measure and perfection and moved into a spirit world of freedom and unrestraint, passing by Satan and the God of the Jews into the kingdom of a Christ that was God, a god of forgiveness of sin, a god encouraging evil and good, a god of Imagination uncontained.

All this Blake accomplished through poetry, painting and vision. In poetry he first followed the Elizabethans; in painting, the Greeks, Florentines and Venetians; in religion, Swedenborg and Boehme. In time he found all schools cramping and threw them off for Imagination, which to him meant Vision.

Blake's outward life was regular and uneventful. But inwardly he early began that experience of the supernatural which was to render his days and nights thrilling and to furnish his pen and brush with "models from eternity". His father was a dissenter, with a leaning towards Swedenborgianism; yet he and the boy's mother were moved at sundry times to chastise their son for declaring persistently that he saw angels in one tree and Ezekiel under others. Later, Blake's wife was better attuned, and liked to remind her husband of how he once saw God at the window.

At fourteen Blake refused to be apprenticed to Ryland, the engraver, because he foresaw that Ryland would be hanged; so his father put him under Basire instead, to remain with him for seven years. Before going to Basire, however, Blake had given his allegiance to Raphael, Michael Angelo and Dürer, whom he early included under his favorite term Gothic, as opposed to the classical tendencies of his time. After two years with Basire, he quarreled with his fellow apprentices over matters of intellectual argument, so he was set to making drawings of Gothic monuments, chiefly in Westminster Abbey. There he was happy. He drove the Westminster boys out of the Temple and had a vision of Christ and the Apostles. Here, too, he was inspired to produce his engraving *Joseph of Arimathea Among the Rocks of Albion* (1773); and probably others now lost.

He left Basire in 1778 and soon made the acquaintance of Flaxman, who was reviving the simple lines of Greek art in his illustrations of the Homeric poems; of Stothard, the painter, and of Fuseli, the engraver, with two of whom he later quarreled. Meantime, in 1780, when he was twenty-three, he exhibited his *Death of Earl Godwin* at the Royal Academy, and in 1784 his *War Unchained by an Angel: Fire, Pestilence and Famine Following,* and his *Abroad in a City: The Morning after a Battle.* The first

Other Essays and Notes

is lost, but the second anticipates his later work in its strength and imaginative power. He escaped the excesses of neo-Michelangelism about this time, according to Russell,[6] by the miscarriage of a plan to send him to Rome. Meantime he was reading Shakespeare, Milton, Dante, Swedenborg and Boehme; and issued in 1783 his *Poetical Sketches,* based not on the neo-classical eighteenth century, but on the romantic Elizabethan age.

From 1783 to 1800 Blake continued to live in different parts of London and produced many works. With the Gothic, the Elizabethan and the visionary manners strong upon him, he added another element to his romantic revolt against his time; namely, political revolution. At Johnson the Bookseller's he met William Godwin, Mary Wollstonecraft and Thomas Paine, famous for their radical theories of government, religion and the family. This group fanned Blake's innate anarchism. *His Marriage of Heaven and Hell,* 1790, proclaimed religious liberty; his *Visions of the Daughters of Albion,* 1793, liberty of the senses; his *French Revolution,* 1791, and his *America,* 1793, political liberty; and his *Europe,* 1794, liberty of the spirit. His other minor prophetical books were also written during this time, and his famous *Songs of Innocence,* 1789, and *Songs of Experience,* 1794; also his comments on Swedenborg and Lavater (for which see Mr. Ellis's *The Real Blake.*) Pictorially, the period was not so rich, but what he did was bought by Thomas Butts, who paid him to produce what he pleased. And though not prolific in painting, this time was of extreme importance to Blake, for it was in 1787 that his brother Robert returned to him in a vision and showed him a method of relief etching,—a crucial moment in his career. As a result, Blake published his *Printed Drawings* in 1788:

[6] "The Letters of William Blake," p. XXIII.

at about the same time he painted some small pictures in oil, not having yet "made up his mind to alienate himself from the influences, Greek, Flemish and Venetian, which were to become so odious to him."⁷ In 1799-1800, in fact, he wrote both to Trusler and Cumberland in a manner of high laudation of Greek art, which he had the insight at this time to include among his romantic enthusiasms. Then his "conversion" began. In 1800, with a part of Butts' patronage, but not his friendship, withdrawn, Blake removed to Felpham to engrave for Hayley. He expected to be freed from drudgery and to work unfettered, or at least to wear light harness gracefully.

But he was unable to bear constraint. He had to do miniatures for the gentry, decorate Hayley's library and read Klopstock and learn Greek with his patron. Hayley had little sympathy with Blake's poems, visions and paintings. Blake soon found that only in London could he live alone with his own spirit, yet he admitted that this "three years' slumber by the banks of ocean" was a settling and a crystallizing period for his ideas. "I have collected", he writes from Felpham, "all my scattered thoughts on art,—which in the confusion of London I had very much obliterated from my mind." Visions swarmed about him at Felpham. He revised *The Four Zoas* and began the composition of *Milton* and *Jerusalem*. Then in September, 1803, he returned to London. "I am drunk with intellectual vision", he wrote to Hayley in 1804, "whenever I take a pencil or graver into my hand, even as I used to be in my youth, and as I have not been for twenty dark but very profitable years." For finally the supreme vision had come. While visiting the Truchesian Picture Gallery, in 1804, Blake cast out " the spectrous fiend Reason" and

[7] A. G. B. Russell: "The Letters of William Blake," p. XXV.

turned once and for all to Imagination. With Reason went all else,—Bacon, Newton, Voltaire, Greek Art,—which is mathematic form,—the Jews, the Italians, Swedenborg, Boehme, Lavater, the eighteenth century, the Elizabethans,—his friends, even, when they opposed him. Blake stood alone upon the world. He completed *Milton* and *Jerusalem*, wrote his *Descriptive Catalogue, Public Address, Last Judgment, The Mental Traveller, The Everlasting Gospel* and *The Death of Abel*. But more important, he painted his great pictures,—among others, his *Canterbury Pilgrims*, his *Vision of the Last Judgment*, his illustrations to Blair's *Grave* and to *Job* and his designs for Dante. All were inspired by Imagination, awakened in him in Westminster Abbey, obscured for him in London, recovered by him at Felpham, and possessing him as a very god in London.

Only with this outline of his spiritual, literary and artistic biography before us, are we prepared to examine and understand his new Christianity.

I

Blake patriotically embodied his vision of Christ in "Albion." There he stood on the brave little island, a bard with streaming hair, clinging to a mountain peak of inspiration, peering into England and through it at all other nations, far back, till he saw and almost touched with his hands the one Eternal Verity, Christianity. Meanwhile the antiquities of the Jews were nothing exceptional to him. *All* nations "had originally one language and one religion; this was the religion of Jesus, the everlasting Gospel. Antiquity preaches the Gospel of Jesus." Jerusalem herself was daughter of Albion and Britannica. "Albion, our ancestor, patriarch of the Atlantic continent, whose history preceded that of the Hebrews, and in whose sleep or chaos creation began" is pictured and described in *The Last Judgment.* Everything existent in Albion and in this world as a whole is an imperfect copy of lost originals, with the sole exception of the Hebrew Bible and the Greek gospels, "which are genuine, preserved by the Saviour's mercy."—Blake's hierarchy, we may add, comprised the Supreme God; Christ his Son; Satan, the Author of Evil; and Urizen, the God of the Jews; the last of whom, according to Mr. Russell in his edition of Blake's *Milton* "had separated himself from the fourfold 'Divine Family,' and exalting his own selfhood, and usurping sovereignty, had endeavored to impose upon man his iron laws, which 'no flesh nor spirit could keep one moment.' "

To Mr. Chesterton, who has written with knowledge and enthusiasm of the poet's virtues and foibles, Blake's private vision of Christ "was the vision of a violent and mysterious being, often indignant and occasionally disdainful."[8] Yet "this 'vision of Christ'," to Swinburne,[9] "though it be to all seeming the 'greatest enemy' of other men's visions, can hardly be regarded as the least significant or beautiful that the religious world has yet been in contact with."

Blake sets forth his conception clearly in *The Everlasting Gospel.* In the Prologue, he writes,[10]

> "The vision of Christ that thou dost see
> Is my Vision's Greatest Enemy.
> Thine has a great hook nose like thine;
> Mine has a snub nose like to mine.
> Thine is the Friend of all Mankind;
> Mine speaks in Parables to the Blind.
> Thine loves the same world that mine hates,
> Thy heaven doors are my Hell Gates."

---

[8] "William Blake," page 144. [9] "William Blake: A Study," Chapter II.
[10] Sampson's "Blake's Poetical Works," 1905, p. 246.

Other Essays and Notes

Then he shows that Christ was not gentle, but stern, even to his parents; that he seized "the God of this World" and "bound Old Satan in his Chain;" that "humility is only doubt;" and that when Jesus humbled himself to the Eternal God, God said in wrath,

> "If thou humblest thyself, thou humblest Me;
> Thou also dwelst in Eternity:
> Thou art a Man, God is no more."

So Christ took on human form subject to temptation, mocked the Jewish Sabbath, turned fishermen to Divines, sent his disciples against Religion and Government, consorted with publicans and

> "Left his Father's trade to roam
> A wandering vagrant without Home;
> And thus he others' labour stole,
> That he might live above control."

Besides he forgave Mary Magdalen; while the voice of God cried

> "To be Good only, is to be
> A God or else a Pharisee."

Lastly, Christ bound in his Being "Satan and all his Hellish Crew," nailed his own Body on the Cross, crucified Nature and the Devil and freed Spirit and Imagination forever.

> "I am sure this Jesus will not do,
> Either for Englishmen or Jew,"

Blake concludes by way of *Epilogue;* thereby recalling his epigram on Fuseli; who alone of men was a Christian, though both Turk and Jew:

> "And so, dear Christian friends, how do you do?"

Other Essays and Notes

II

Why, we may ask, if we ask it reverently, did Blake not go one step further and say Christ was not coldly ascetic? The reply is a question: why in view of his liberal theories did Blake not indulge himself more freely? Because he worked incessantly, reveled in vision and had for wife the most watchful as she was the most devoted of guardians in literary annals.—In his *Africa*, at least, Blake shows Christ to be a victim of Urizen, the God of this World, who was forced finally to raise up Mohammed to people a world decimated by Christianity. Mr. John P. R. Wallis,[11] in a useful attempt to trace the stages of Blake's Christianity, concludes from *Africa* and *Europe* that Blake began with a hostile attitude towards Christianity, but later made Christ the centre of his system, interpreting the Incarnation, the Crucifixion and the Resurrection in his own mystical way: to the effect, namely, that Christ was born into the world to carry to men the message of the falsity of the senses; that his body was crucified as the symbol of the delusiveness of flesh; and that his spirit rose to Eternity to symbolize the triumph of spirit over death, to be deified there as the supreme artist and the embodiment of humanity and imagination. I believe Mr. Wallis should distinguish throughout between hostility towards orthodox or historical Christianity and Blake's own conception, which, it is true, he only worked out with time, but which was early growing in him. Of the Christ of the Churches he was always as much the foe as he was the champion of his Christ of the Imagination.

---

[11] "Blake's Symbolism and Some of its Recent Interpreters" ("Primitiae," University of Liverpool, 1912).

Other Essays and Notes

III

In *Jerusalem, To the Public,* forgiveness is insisted on; for "the Spirit of Jesus is continual forgiveness of sin: he who waits to be righteous before he enters into the Saviour's kingdom, the Divine Body, will never enter there. I am perhaps the most sinful of men! I pretend not to holiness! Yet I pretend to love, to see, to converse with daily, as man to man, and the more to have an interest in the Friend of Sinners."

How forgiveness is greater than law *The Gates of Paradise* proves; for

"Mutual forgiveness of each vice
Such are the Gates of Paradise,
Against the Accuser's chief desire,
Who walked among the stones of fire.
Jehovah's fingers wrote the Law:
He wept; then rose in zeal and awe,
And, in the midst of Sinai's heat,
Hid it beneath His Mercy-seat.
 O Christians! Christians! tell me why
You rear it on your altars high!"

In his *Blake's Religious Lyrics* (*Essays and Studies by Members of the English Association,* vol. III, Oxford, 1912) H. C. Beeching adduces passages from Blake on forgiveness and confesses that he does not understand how the poet expects forgiveness to act. He neglects to apply what he sets forth clearly enough earlier: that Blake allowed himself and anyone else to sin, with the assurance that Christ would forgive; that by sinning, by forgiving and being forgiven men attain that continuously new selfhood which to Blake was growth away from the old selfhood of Satan and the God of this World towards the real selfhood of Christ and the true God. When Beeching wonders whether Blake had forgiven those enemies of his whom he flayed in his epigrams, he forgets that to Blake "these fellows," as he calls them elsewhere, were serving the God of the Jews or Satan, were therefore Pharisees or the damned, were contracted selves and consequently not among the number he or Christ forgave, until they repented.

Obviously, then, Blake held to the doctrine of Freewill in sinning. True, Erin says in *Jerusalem*:[12]

> 'Learn therefore, O Sisters, to distinguish the
>   Eternal Human
> That walks about among the stones of fire, in bliss
>   and woe
> Alternate, from those States or Worlds in which the
>   Spirit travels:
> This is the only means to Forgiveness of Enemies.'

But with this aspect of his theory of States we must compare and contrast the *Sequel to the Last Judgment*, where we find that the persistently self-righteous perish, till they repent; for, "All life consists of these two, throwing off error and knaves from our company continually, and receiving truth, or wise men into our company continually. . . . When any individual rejects error and embraces truth, a Last Judgment passes upon that individual. . . . The fool shall not enter into Heaven be he ever so holy. . . . I do not consider either the just or the unjust or the wicked to be in a supreme state, but to be every one of them states of that sleep which the soul may fall into in its deadly dreams of good and evil when it leaves Paradise following the serpent. . . . The accuser is cast out not because he sins but because he torments the just."

Another writer who touches on Blake's Christianity is Caroline T. E. Spurgeon in *Mysticism in English Literature*, Cambridge University Press, 1913. "It is easy to

[12] See Arthur Symon's "William Blake," p. 178.

Other Essays and Notes

see," says the writer, "that this faculty which Blake calls 'Imagination' entails of itself naturally and inevitably the Christian doctrine of self-sacrifice." As a matter of fact, neither Blake nor his vision of Christ are self-sacrificing in the Christian sense. According to Blake, he, and Christ before him, were not unselfish for others' sakes, but for their own. What they strove for was not unselfishness at all, but multiplicity of selfhoods,—a continual withdrawal from a hard-bound self into ever-changing selves that approach nearer and nearer to God. In *To the Deists* Blake shows that man is by nature evil. "Man is born a Spectre or Satan," says he, "and is altogether an Evil, and requires a New Selfhood continually, and must continually be changed into his direct contrary. Without contraries," he continues in *The Marriage of Heaven and Hell*, "is no progression. Attraction and repulsion, reason and energy, love and hate, are necessary to human existence." Entire liberty of action in the physical world and unfettered Imagination in the spiritual brought men, to Blake, into oneness with Christ and God. When men refused to renew their selfhoods continually by breaking the chains both of Satan and the God of this world, or declined to be enlightened by Christ or Blake, they were unworthy of self-sacrifice from a seer and did not receive it. The just in God's eyes and the wicked in men's — these enter Heaven: but those who sit in judgment in this world — the just in Man's eyes, followers of the God of this world, and the wicked in the true God's sight, Satan's crew — these are hypocrites and Pharisees and sinners and are burned in Hell-fires until they repent.

IV

In the fastnesses of his soul, therefore, Blake was a supreme egoist. Too many critics insist on seeing him in terms of our common life instead of walking alone with him and his mysteries. Often Blake wrote simply; such passages are comprehensible; to persons he was courteous. But these moments were sops to Cerberus that he might pass on into his own Elysium. There he dwelt with Imagination and with one other, his wife, who could follow after him and share his vision.

Yet M. Berger says, "His doctrine was the very essence of Christianity; the doctrine of the love of all men, to which he adds, as the Indian sages did, that of self-forgetfulness and love of all nature. He who advocated the sanctity of men's desires and the lawfulness of their complete satisfaction, undoes, by a strange contradiction, the sacrifice of those very desires, not through obedience to a tyrannical law, but solely through love and abnegation of self." His references are to *Jerusalem*, p. 96 and to *Milton*, p. 39, wherein Brotherhood and Self-annihilation are mentioned, apparently with orthodox Christian connotations. Albion and Milton say they live to do kindness to their brothers and to annihilate themselves for others' good, alike for Christ's sake and for Satan's, for good men's and for evil. In the last scene of *Jerusalem*, again, even Bacon, Newton and Locke are saved. Yet this annihilation of one's self, to Blake, is effected for growth towards spiritual truth of each individual. It is as the individual approaches nearer and nearer to Truth, and rids himself of Error, that he is able to help others. Blake's brotherhood and self-sacrifice are enlightened selfishness; one's own spiritual growth, by successions of selfhoods, is the growth of others, since it points them the way to Salvation.

In this connection a curious but not inexplicable aspect of Blake's theology is his theory of the Last Judgment,

Other Essays and Notes

from which we have already quoted. "A Last Judgment is necessary because fools flourish," says he. "Forgiveness of sin is only at the judgment seat of Jesus, the Saviour, where the accuser is cast out not because he sins, but because he torments the just. . . . The Last Judgment is an overwhelming of bad art and science. Some people flatter themselves that there will be no Last Judgment, and that bad art will be adopted and mixed with good art, that error, or experiment, will make a part of truth, and they boast that it is its foundation. These people flatter themselves. I will not flatter them. Error is created. Truth is eternal. Error or creation will be burned.—It is burned up the moment men come to behold it."

Blake believed in Truth as ardently as Plato, but it was his own vision of Truth, and he wanted to impress it upon the world as irresistibly as Socrates and Christ did their conceptions. He called the outward world "dirt upon my feet — no part of me." Imagination and Vision were eternal. "The Last Judgment", says he "will be when all those are cast away who trouble religion with questioning concerning good or evil, or eating of the tree of those knowledges and reasonings which hinder the vision of God, turning all into a consuming fire. When imagination, art and science, and all intellectual gifts—all the gifts of the Holy, Ghost — are looked upon as of no use, and only contention remains to man, then the Last Judgment begins, and its vision is seen by every eye according to the situation which he holds."

Mr. Ellis[13] refers to " the contrast and seeming antagonism between the sweetness of Blake's religious professions and the fury of his denunciations of those who, he

---

[13] "The Real Blake," p. 329.

thought, had used him ill." Yet " 'does not Jesus,' he reflected, 'whom we are told to imitate, promise in the end to cast off forever all who will not accept him? In his parables is not the tree, that by a year's gardening is proved useless, to be cut down? Did he not whip his own enemies out of his 'Father's House?' 'He that is not with me is against me,' with the postscript — 'and I will be against him' was Blake's Christianity." Here are frank admissions on Mr. Ellis's part; but why still cling to "the sweetness of Blake's religous professions?" Blake formed his system not out of sweetness, but to save his own soul, then others'! And with profound benevolence he *forgave* everybody who disagreed with him, because all are in *states* till they see what Blake saw. For all men "to be in error and to be cast out is part of God's plan" (Ellis, p. 421). "Some are born to endless night; it is right it should be so."

"Yet towards the last," says Ellis, p. 431 "his mind was coming to understand that even folly might not exclude us from heaven forever." In 1827 Blake wrote to Cumberland, "Flaxman is gone, and we must all follow soon, everyone to his Own Eternal Home, leaving the Delusive Goddess Nature to her Laws, to get into Freedom from all Law of the Numbers, into the Mind, in which everyone is King and Priest in his own Home. God send it on Earth as it is in Heaven." The tone is gentle here, yet it still has tolerance chiefly for the saved in Blake's eyes. But no doubt even the condemned will have many other chances in the cycles. "The world of imagination", he writes in *The Last Judgment,* "is a world of reality. It is the divine bosom into which we shall all go after the death of the vegetated body. This world of imagination is infinite and eternal, whereas the world of generation or vegetation is finite and temporal. There exist in that eternal world the eternal realities of everything which we see reflected in this vegetable glass of nature." The quality of eternity is perfect truth and undertaking, from which man fell, and to which he returns in proportion to the rapidity with which he grasps Imagination and Vision and ceases to believe in the verity of Nature and the senses. When he has returned to the primal state, Reason and Feeling will be merged in Imagination; yet even so, these will continue contending in him, giving him clearer and profounder knowledge of the nature of God and Christ, knowledge of whom — and of man—is of infinite possibility. For I cannot agree with Dr. Pierce[14] that perfect balance was what Blake preached for his ideal man. Rather I think he expected men to go on contending and growing till the end of time, if not eternally. M. Berger says of the former (p. 130), "Before the beginning of Time they (the Zoas) were united in the universal brotherhood of Eden, and at the end of Time they will be united again for all eternity. Meanwhile, it is their struggles and their changing fortunes that make our world what it is: the dream-filled sleep of Man upon the Rock of Ages." With Dr. Pierce's permission, there is no harmony and balance in man here until the end of Time, if even then; whereas he holds that Blake preached it for earth. Blake desired spiritual conflict on earth, not peace. Spiritual peace was aeons beyond, and seen but with the imaginative eye.

V

Of interest, finally, to our inquiry, are traces of affinity in Blake with our own planet and time. He was a pioneer in English romanticism,[15] and English romanticism still

[14] Introduction to his "Selections from the Symbolical Poems of William Blake," 1915.
[15] See Dorothea Melinda Melden's "Romantic Traits and Tendencies in the Literary Work of William Blake," (Master's Thesis, The University of California, 1914.)

lives. Are some of his favorite notions, now that romanticism has caught up with him, more generally abroad? I think there are several. For example, Blake's romantic forgiveness of sinners has a modern ring. Our sentimental contention, again, that when we sin in man's sight we do not sin in God's, appears in *To the Christians*. "He who despises and mocks a Mental Gift in another, calling it pride and selfishness and sin, mocks Jesus the giver of every Mental Gift, which always appear to the ignorance-loving Hypocrite as Sins: but that which is a sin in the sight of cruel man, is not so in the sight of our kind God."

The Divine Image, on the other hand, is a noble and poetical exaltation of man into fellowship with an anthropomorphic Deity, but it is found in the *Songs of Innocence*:

"To Mercy, Pity, Peace and Love,
  All pray in their distress,
And to these virtues of delight
  Return their thankfulness.

For Mercy, Pity, Peace and Love
  Is God our Father dear;
And Mercy, Pity, Peace and Love
  Is man, His child and care.

For Mercy has a human heart;
  Pity a human face;
And Love, the human form divine;
  And Peace, the human dress.

Then every man, of every clime,
  That prays in his distress,
Prays to the human form divine;
  Love, Mercy, Pity, Peace.

And all must love the human form,
  In heathen, Turk, or Jew,
Where Mercy, Love, and Pity dwell,
  There God is dwelling too."

Other Essays and Notes

In the *Songs of Experience*, in which Blake sets forth the world we live in, as contrasted with the ideal world of the *Songs of Innocence*, *The Divine Image* is parodied in *The Human Abstract*.

"Pity would be no more
If we did not make somebody poor,"

says he. In *The Songs of Experience*, again, he anticipates the nineteenth and twentieth centuries in their sympathy for children who toil,—or study.

The Little Vagabond makes application of Blake's easy-going theories to the Church, and embodies, with grim exaggeration, our current notion that the Church should be warmer, pleasanter and more human. If you would have us exchange the ale-house for the church, says the impish Vagabond, give us some of the prerogatives of the ale-house. A like case is modern education, where "holding the child in school," especially the odd one, takes the form of allowing him to amuse himself, retain his peculiarities and express his impulses, under guidance. Blake thought little of guidance himself. He lacked formal education, and was glad of it; and his culture was acquired as a concomitant to his writing and painting.[16] "He wanted supremacy of freedom with intensity of faith," says Swinburne. To be both a Christian and a Pagan was as essential to him as poetry and painting. Such a life as Blake's, as Mr. Benson observes in his *Essays*,[17] was an attempt at reconciling the equally tyrannical claims upon Man of Beauty and of Religion.

But Blake substituted feeling for judgment, and called Imagination justice. He did not *sympathize* with evil, he *advocated* evil, that Christ might forgive and that man

[16] W. M. Rossetti: "Blake's Poetical Works," pp. XIV-XV.
[17] pp. 178-9.

might obtain salvation. He forgot Paul's admonition to the Romans. "What shall we say then? Shall we continue in sin, that grace may abound? God forbid!" Indeed, Beeching's emphasis on the Pauline element in Blake does not strike us as sound. On the contrary, "Paul will be read of in Blake along with Constantine, Charlemagne and Luther, as one who was not a whole-hearted upholder of Forgiveness as the only Christ," says Ellis.[18]

Richard Le Gallienne[19] is impressed with the exquisite simplicity and perfection of true Christianity, and declares the world has never yet tested the Gospel. Professor Royce finds a simple return to primitive Christianity inadequate.[20] To Eucken[21] Christianity is a "a progressive historic movement still in the making." Meredith saw Christ oftenest righteously angry and scourging folly. These men are all reverent. In his vision of Jesus, Blake was not. A world of Pharisees had embittered him, hence his conception of Christ is not lovely. His idea of Jesus distorts the Christian theories of forgiveness, sacrifice, and salvation. Of course his precise relation to changing Christianity remains problematical; on the whole, however, to understand his Christianity is to abandon it. Smethan[22] turns sadly away from it without even examining it. Beeching and Spurgeon and others read orthodoxy into it.

In that chaotic, mystical volume, too radical for the orthodox, too orthodox for the radical, *The Finality of Christianity*, Prof. George Burman Foster writes:

[18] "The Real Blake," p. 352.
[19] "The Religion of a Literary Man."
[20] "What Is Vital in Christianity?" ("Harvard Theological Review," II, p. 342).
[21] "Can We Still Be Christians?" Translated by Lucy Judge Gibson, 1914, p. 218.
[22] "Literary Works," p. 145, ed. by Wm. Davies, 1913.

Other Essays and Notes

"Not to shrink back from the indispensable but perilous task of releasing the gold from the dross, the kernel from the shell, the gospel in its purity and simplicity from time historical beliefs — that is the duty of the hour, a duty which no calumny and ridicule, no loss and no cross, should prevent the lover of his kind from consummating."[23]

Blake himself did not shrink back; he was unafraid; he found Christianity the divinest thing in the universe; but for a Christ meek, lowly, long-suffering and at peace, he substituted a Christ proud, haughty, imperious and warlike. Something of the vigor of his conception is undoubtedly entering into our modern visions; most of its wrath has happily evaporated. Even the warring nations are calling upon the Father, not upon the Son.

---

[23] For something in the same strain see Mr. Edward Garnett's "Mr. George Moore's New Christ," a review of "The Brook Kerith" ("The Dial," Sept. 21, 1916). The review of the book in the September "Academy," 1916, and the "Nation" of October 19, 1916 — "Moore's the Pity" and "George Moore as Interpreter of Jesus" — are stinging criticisms of Moore and his works generally.

IV

The Influence of William Blake on William Butler Yeats

SWINBURNE understood Blake, but did not imitate his mysticism. Wordsworth and Coleridge appreciated him, but did not follow him. I doubt if Pater or Francis Thompson ever penetrated far into his Prophetical Books, though the enthusiasm of both for Blake is well known; and when Bliss Carman celebrates him in *By the Aurelian Well and Other Elegies* it is under the title *The Country of Har, for the Centenary of Blake's Songs of Innocence.* Mr. Shaw's new Christianity, in his Preface (1915) to *Androcles and the Lion,* has marked affinities with Blake's when he writes "Gentle Jesus, meek and mild is a snivelling modern invention, with no warrant in the Gospel"; or when he is composing the section which he calls *The Savage John and the Civilized Jesus;* but I see no evidence that he drew directly upon Blake; especially since it is Communism which he sees essentially in Christianity, and preaches. The New Christianity of Mr. George Moore's *Brook Kerith,* 1916, again, is forged only in part out of Blake's: for it mainly continues Mr. Shaw's attack on Paulinistic Christianity; but to the extent of having Christ rise again to abjure his proud claims as Messiah and the Son of God and to continue his life quietly as a humble shepherd.

But all agree that Yeats has been somehow influenced by Blake. With Mr. Ellis he made an exhaustive study of the Prophetical Books for their great three-volume edition of Blake, 1893. Mr. Moore's *Ave* is filled with Yeats and

Other Essays and Notes

Blake, and tells (p. 47) how Moore and Yeats argued over the *Book of Tiel* (shouldn't it read Thel?) and how Yeats lined his walls with Blake engravings. Yeats' *Ideas of Good and Evil* takes its title from Blake,[24] and assigns two papers to him, with other references. *The Cutting of an Agate* refers to Blake a half dozen times. Like Blake, Mr. Yeats admits that he "sees" things; and like Blake, again, he is fond of distinguishing between allegory and vision; or as he prefers to call it, symbolism. His imagination is of Blake's intuitive type, though less powerful, and has much of Blake's clearness of outline; as compared, at least, with Maeterlinck's vaguer abstractive symbolism.

Yeats was conversant with Oriental mysticism and Irish spirits before he knew Blake's Prophetical Books, as we learn from the Preface to Volume I of the Ellis-Yeats edition. Yet his later intensive study of Blake deepened his susceptibility to Vision and Imagination. "The mysticism which is implicit in the poems becomes explicit and definite in certain books of prose," says Eugene Mason in *The Poet as Mystic; William Butler Yeats (A Book of Preferences in Literature,* 1915). These prose volumes are *The Celtic Twilight,* 1893, *Ideas of Good and Evil,* 1903, and *The Cutting of an Agate,* 1912. "Art and Poetry", says the Ellis-Yeats Preface, "by constantly using symbolism, continually remind us that nature itself is a symbol. To remember this is to be redeemed from nature's death and destruction. This is Blake's message." *The Celtic Twilight* describes a Visionary[25] reminding one much of

---

[24] See "The Poems of William Blake," edited by W. B. Yeats, p. 241. (The Muses' Library).

[25] Mentioned again in "Ideas of Good and Evil" (in "Speaking to the Psaltery," II) and coupled there with Blake and his "Songs of Innocence." In "Edmund Spenser," IX ("The Cutting of an Agate," 1912) Yeats adds, "I find that though I love symbolism, which is often the only fitting speech for some mystery of disembodied life, I am for the most part bored by allegory, which is made, as Blake says, 'by the daughters of memory,' and coldly, with no wizard frenzy."

Blake, for he sees, paints, and writes about vision. This man (who is, I daresay, A. E.) is peculiarly Celtic, according to Yeats,—who believes, by the way, that Blake was Irish. Mr. Symons takes issue with that in his book on Blake.— Another section of *The Celtic Twilight*,— *A Voice*, discloses Yeats himself seeing a vision, but not a fantastic vision,—which he says is not the primary quality of Irish imagination,—but a beautiful mild vision, "peaceful like the faces of animals." The terror of Blake's figures is not in Yeats' visions, which are rarified and refined. He does not see ghosts of fleas. Yet one of his Irishmen in *The Celtic Twilight* declares in Blake's vein, "I have seen Hell myself. I had sight of it one time in a vision." The dreaminess of Yeats', as compared with the realism of Blake's vision, is brought out in the book by Yeats' reference to "bodiless moods" and by his question, "What is literature but the expression of moods by the vehicle of symbol or incident?"

"All sounds, all colours, all forms, either because of their pre-ordained energies or because of long association, evoke indefinable yet precise emotions, or, as I prefer to think, call down among us certain disembodied powers, whose footsteps over our hearts we call emotions," he writes in *The Symbolism of Poetry* (*Ideas of Good and Evil*). In *The Moods* (*idem*) he follows Blake in holding that argument, theory, erudition, and reason are means, not ends,— illusions, Yeats says, "to serve the moods." Mood is too weak a word for Blake, who would say Imagination. Yeats sees some such difference in himself and Blake in his Magic, VI (*id.*), when he writes, "What matter 'if God himself only acts or is in existing beings or men', as Blake believed? We must none the less admit that invisible beings, far wandering influences, shapes that may have floated from a hermit in the wilderness, brood over council-chambers and studies and battle-fields." The contrast between Blake's power of sight and Yeats' comes out at the end of *Symbolism in Painting (id.)*, in which a brilliant passage from Blake, describing his visionary sense, is quoted and followed by an example of Yeats's own experience of a troop of blue people who appeared to him with little roses embroidered on their robes. In *William Blake and His Illustrations*, indeed, Yeats says Blake was "a too literal realist of the imagination, as others are of nature." He was a symbolist, again, "who had to invent his symbols," who, if he had gone to Ireland for them would have chosen "the sacred mountains, along whose sides the peasant still sees enchanted fires."

What Yeats gets especially from Blake is his theory that Imagination is greater than Reason. "I have observed dreams and visions very carefully," he writes in *The Philosophy of Shelley's Poetry*, and I am now certain that the imagination has some way of lighting on the truth that the reason has not, and that its commandments, delivered when the body is still and the reason silent, are the most binding we can ever know." In *Discoveries: The Subject Matter of Drama* we learn that experience is water, emotion, wine. *The Black and White Arrows (Discoveries)* with its refrain of Instinct versus Reason may well be quoted entire; for "instinct," according to Yeats, "creates the recurring and the beautiful, all the winding of the serpent; but reason, the most ugly man, as Blake called it, is the drawer of the straight line, the maker of the arbitrary and the impermanent, for no recurring spring will ever bring again yesterday's clock. Sanctity has its straight line also, darting from the centre, and with these arrows the many-coloured serpent, theme of all our poetry, is maimed and hunted. He that finds the white arrow shall have wisdom older than the serpent, but what of the black arrow? How much knowledge, how heavy a quiver of the crow-feathered ebony can the soul endure?"

The result of all this is admirably expressed by Forrest Reid in his *W. B. Yeats; A Critical Study,* p. 214. Like his philosophy, Yeats' mystic morality "reveals an aspect of the truth, but if we ask if it is a revelation of the whole of truth it fails signally. For this reason, perhaps, it comes to us more convincingly, certainly more persuasively, when it is still merely intuitive." Trained intuitionally by Blake, Yeats follows Shelley in his search for the eternal beauty; which both attain intellectually as well as emotionally, by the way. " 'Go put off holiness and put on intellect!' cries Blake, and Owen Aherne and Michael Robartes echo that cry, though in other moods Mr. Yeats may make a paradox about the wisdom of fools," writes Mr. Reid, (page 218). After all, Blake and Shelley "used their heads", and Mr. Yeats does, too, to write such exquisitely finished poetry and prose as he does; but Yeats loves dreams best, moods next, thought last.

Among Yeats' plays only one shows strong marks of Blake. This is the prose drama *Where There is Nothing;* which has for its hero Paul Ruttledge, a man who scorns laws, philosophies, institutions, the Church and Reason. Strip the Ibsen, the Irish, the Borrowian, and the Yeats' elements from Paul, and the residue is Blake reincarnated.[26] Paul is a country gentleman who desires to "live above control", so he goes wandering with tinkers and marries one of their number. Sabina is as devoted to him as

[26] Later, in his Preface to "The Unicorn from the Stars," Mr. Yeats repudiated Paul Ruttledge as a character conceived in haste and repented at leisure. "The Unicorn from the Stars" is Lady Gregory's rewriting of "Where There is Nothing."

Other Essays and Notes

Catherine Blake was to Blake, but unlike Catherine, she retains but small hold on him; he leaves her, and dies unconscious of her presence. But Paul has Blake in mind in Act III when he says, "Some poet has written that exuberance is beauty, and that the roadway of excess leads to the palace of wisdom". "As I can't leap from cloud to cloud", he says in Blake's vein, "I want to wander from road to road." In his reference in Act III to the old impossible saying of turning the other cheek, he has Blake in mind again; as when Blake says, for example,

> "He has observed the golden rule
> Till he's become the golden fool".

There is much talk throughout the piece about getting away from law and number. "I have learned," says Paul, "that one needs a religion so wholly supernatural, that is so opposed to the order of nature, that the world can never capture it."

The hero attacks Newton in Act I, and in his great speech in Act IV declares the Laws were the first sin; that "everything that desires" is full of God's will. "The Christian's business is not reformation but revelation," he declares. He attacks the churches, and says Christ came to overthrow government and all settled order. In the last act he turns upon organized reform, and declares, again in Blakean terms, "God will accomplish his last judgment, first in one man's mind and then in another. He is always planning last judgments. And yet it takes a long time, and that is why he laments in the wind and in the reeds and in the cries of the curlews." "At death," says he, "the soul comes into possession of itself, and returns to the joy that made it". Finally he expresses Blake's nihilism in an extreme form in the words, "We must destroy the World; we must destroy everything that has Law and Number, *for where there is nothing, there is God.*" This coveted region he defines in *Where There is Nothing* (*The Secret Rose*) as the void beyond the nine crystalline spheres.

In his *William Blake*, M. Berger has said that "Mr. Yeats has made us feel through his poems as if much of the spirit of our great mystic were again living in him." I cannot see much direct influence myself on Yeats as a poet. Aedh, Hanrahan and Michael Robartes of *The Secret Rose* are symbols of moods; oftener Mr. Yeats takes his symbols from sun, moon, trees, flowers and animals. *The Wind Among the Reeds,* 1899, is most symbolic, and disparages reality. In these poems "woman is an unwitting messenger from the world of immortals, bringing word of immortal desires, and urging the lover to long for the end of Time and Birth and Change; and happy are those who understand with Blake that the passions are the angels of God."[27]

I fancy that Yeats' early poems drew some of their simplicity from Blake's *Songs of Innocence,* but I cannot prove the point. He doesn't say so in his *Reveries over Childhood and Youth,* 1916. Surely his fairies are Ireland's. They are philosophical fairies, though, in whose company we are consciously free.[28]—As for Yeats' epigrams and later realistic work in *The Green Helmet* and *Responsibilities,*—they are parallels, at times, but nothing more, to Blake's petulant utterances of like sort. Both men — Blake in his struggle for existence, Yeats in his experience with the management of his theatre — are mystics who awake with a shock when they strike upon the rocks of

---

[27] J. M. Hone: "William Butler Yeats," p. 57.
[28] See "The Living Age," vol. 276, p. 483.

that reality which they would have us feel elsewhere is illusion. Yet that illusion, in spite of his new manner, is what the world still looks for in Yeats,—the fairies, the wise fools, the aspiring souls of his early and middle poems, of his poetical dramas and of *Where There is Nothing,*—not the bitterness of his epigrams, not the annoyances of real men and women, not the new *Hour Glass* of the *Responsibilities,* not the revised *Where There is Nothing* of *The Unicorn from the Stars.* After all, when Yeats' writing is done, the scholar he mentions in his *Philosophy of Shelley's Poetry* as more intellectual than intuitive, may yet do him the service of collating his texts and pointing out which is his true work and which are his concessions to the world of natural things and to that Ireland which he nobly serves.

V

William Vaughn Moody's Feeling for the Seventeenth Century

WILLIAM VAUGHN MOODY'S characterization of the temperament of his friend Trumbull Stickney (*North American Review*, Vol. 183, p. 1005) as "a solid rock basis of Puritanism covered with the flowers and vines of a pagan sensibility, and interpenetrated as by veins of fire with a passionate poetic imagination" is quite as applicable to his own. "You have only to scratch a Cavalier ever so lightly to find below the surface a Puritan in full theological panoply," says Professor Manly in his Introduction to the Poems and Plays of Moody. Moody was born and reared a Puritan. But he "fused his ancient cosmology and theology with his evolutionary theories, recharactered his God, as so many of us have done, and achieved a poetic solution of the universe," continues Mr. Manly. Elsewhere in the essay the same writer speaks of "the union of religious mysticism and joy in the sensuous life which is the dominant note of all Moody's later work."

The Greek, the Hebraic, the Christian, the Oriental, the Mediæval, the French, the German, the Italian, the English and the American strains are either quite apparent in Moody's work, or are pointed out by Mr. Manly in his Introduction. What is a little less on the surface, or what at least we do not yet find emphasized, is the influence on Moody of the English seventeenth century. Mr. Charlton M. Lewis, for instance, in a study of Moody in the *Yale Review*, July, 1913, allies the poet, to

Other Essays and Notes

some extent, with the symbolists, and points out the influence in his work of Leopardi, Léon Dierx, Shelley, the Pre-Raphaelites, Arnold, Coventry Patmore, and Trumbull Stickney. But Milton and the seventeenth century are not mentioned.

Yet Moody's pieces of scholarly and critical work, *The Complete Poetical Works of John Milton* (Cambridge Edition) and Bunyan's *Pilgrim's Progress*, fall in the seventeenth century. Again, his chapter on *The Seventeenth Century: Non-dramatic Literature Before the Restoration*, in Moody and Lovett's *A History of English Literature*[29] is a triumph in condensation and appreciation of the spirit of the period. And the poem *Thammuz* owed its suggestion to *Paradise Lost*.

In his *Ode in Time of Hesitation* the poet turns instinctively to Milton:

> "Are we the eagle nation Milton saw
> Mewing its mighty youth,
> Soon to possess the mountain winds of truth,
> And be a swift familiar of the sun
> Where aye before God's face his trumpets run?"

"When at last his duty as a patriot was done, he turned at once to his deferred task," says Moody of Milton and his Epic. So, when Moody had written his *Ode* and his lyrics; when he had taught English and written his plays, he could turn to the completion of his Trilogy; namely, his *Fire-Bringer*, his *Masque of Judgment* and his *Death of Eve*. Of this work William Morton Payne writes in the *Dial*, 53, 484: "It is Milton's attempt to 'justify the ways of God to man' coupled with the attempt of the later poets to justify the ways of man to God. It is the Great Syn-

---

[29] "I am working now on the Milton period; have it something more than half done," Moody writes, Aug. 18, 1900, to Robert Morss Lovett, whose mastery of the seventeenth century is only second to Moody's own.

thesis undertaken by the emancipated modern spirit, the fusing of God and his world into a monistic system." To this, however, we add Professor Manly's qualifying words: "Moody's conception of God was not, for all his insistence upon the inseparableness of God and man, pantheistic." May Sinclair, in the *Atlantic*, 98, 1906, calls him "the poet of revolt against spiritual immensities"; but also "the poet of reconciliation and reconstruction".

The choice of the term Masque[30] for his poem recalls Moody's words on *Comus*: "It was characteristic of Milton that he should have put a serious moral lesson into a form of spectacular and lyric entertainment usually of the most frivolous kind. Fortunately, his power as an artist was so developed that he could charge the delicate texture of his masque with ethical doctrine, without at all marring its airy beauty."

The statement applies equally to *The Masque of Judgment*. Moreover, "In the approved epic manner," he says of *Paradise Lost*, "Milton opens his poem in the middle of the action, after the rebellious angels have been cast down into Hell. The earlier events are given in retrospective narrative by the archangel Raphael and Adam." Moody opens the *Masque of Judgment* with a Prelude, spoken by Raphael, Uriel, two shepherds, a boy and a girl. Its tone is at once reminiscent of *Comus;* it is youthful, pastoral, and lyrical. As narrative, however, it is retrospective. Without specific reference it sums up the motives of the *Fire-Bringer*, which, like Milton, begins without prelude, "in the middle of the action."

[30] In a letter to Ferdinand Schevill, Venice, June 8th, 1897, Moody writes, "I am at work now on a rather hopelessly fantastic thing, I fear, half-lyric, half-dramatic; I shall try to excuse the willfulness of the form by calling it a Masque." Moody wrote the "Masque of Judgment" and edited Milton during the years 1897-1900. (See D. G. Mason's "Some Letters of William Vaughn Moody"). In the same letter to Schevill Moody calls the "Masque" a "kind of Hebrew Götterdämerung." Professor Manly compares the poem to a mediaeval *mystere*.

Other Essays and Notes

As Professor Manly points out, the parts of the Trilogy were not written in their logical order. If the *Prelude to the Masque of Judgment* embodies the spirit of *Comus* (and throughout we recall Moody's words on Milton, "He learned how to borrow without imitation"); if the *Masque of Judgment* proper is inspired in part by *Comus*, by *Paradise Lost*, by Blake and others, then the *Fire-Bringer* is Moody's effort "to bring over into English the gravity and calm dignity of the Greek tragedies," as it was Milton's in *Samson Agonistes*. Finally, the *Death of Eve* is Miltonic and more: it strives to embody the spiritual struggles and the spiritual victories of the ages since the greater poet wrote.

Miltonic, too, is the dread charge in the *Daguerreotype*:

> "Take your eyes from me, leave me to my shame,
> Or else if gaze they must,
> Steel them with judgment, darken them with blame;
> But by the ways of light ineffable
> You bade me go and I have faltered from,
> By the low waters moaning out of hell
> Whereto my feet have come
> Lay not on me those intolerable
> Looks of rejoicing love, of pride, of happy trust!"

The *Daguerreotype*, furthermore, though it is much admired, errs in some degree on the very side of the vices with which Moody charges the young Milton and the seventeenth century; namely, "conceitfulness, exaggeration and tasteless ingenuity." The tortured outpourings of the poet before the childlike earnestness and grace of his mother at seventeen are not quite manly; certain lines have Donne outdone, while the comparison of his "bringingsin, his doings-fine" to broken wine-jars, whence "the stale breath sickens, reeking from the shard" are conceited, strained and in imagery out of keeping with the face he gazes on. For truer, more classic grace we turn from *The Daguerreotype* to *Faded Pictures*.

Better taste, too, characterizes *Until the Troubling of the Waters*. Yet that sincere admirer of Moody's poetry, May Sinclair observes,[31] "In this the imagination is superb, the psychology audacious and *on the whole overstrained*. And yet," she continues, "we get the sharp vibrating human note in this poem and in one other, *The Daguerreotype*, in which imagination and emotion are fused. . . . His quality is opulence, a certain gorgeousness, that is never barbaric, owing to his power of classic restraint."

Miss Sinclair's criticism of the two poems is true of Moody's style generally. That "drowning out by the music of an over full orchestra" which many of us feel is one characteristic of Moody, Miss Sinclair explains indirectly in another sentence. "He is an exile in New York," says she, "hungering for the beautiful and spiritual lands." Moody was modern, American, most spiritually minded, part and apart from an age of great issues, of injustice to the poor, of exaltation of the worthy and the unworthy. He escaped, in several ways;— for one, he threw himself into a century with all the fervor and color of our own, but with a spirituality excelling it.

Yet no one who has drunk at the fountain of seventeenth century English is fascinated by its spirituality only. What did John Donne embody, that he should found a school and still attract Moody and the modern world? Professor Saintsbury tells us in the *Introduction* to Donne's

---

[31] "Atlantic," vol. 98.

Other Essays and Notes

Poems, the *Muses Library*, p. xxiv. "It is indeed possible," says he, "that the union of the sensual, intellectual, poetical and religious temperaments is not so very rare; but it is rarely voiceful. That it existed in Donne preëminently, and that it found voice in him as it never has done before or since, no one who knows his life or works can doubt." "His nature was extraordinarily complex," says Charles Eliot Norton in his edition of the *Love Poems of John Donne*, p. vi. "Heaven and earth contended in it with a force that made life a succession of alternating exaltation and depression, loftiness and baseness, rapture and despair. His work, whether in prose or verse, is the expression of a powerful intelligence, a passionate temperament and a vivid imagination irregularly subject to the check of a keen, practical understanding."

In *Song-Flower and Poppy*, II, *At Assisi*, Moody sings:

> "Too purged of earth's good glee and strife
> Too drained of the honied lusts of life,
> Was the peace these old saints won!
>
> * * * * * *
>
> Men build and plan, but the soul of man
> Coming with haughty eyes to scan,
> Feels richer, wilder need."

Richer, wilder need, saints still thrilling with the love of life are our legacy from English seventeenth century poets and churchmen,—Milton, Bunyan, Donne, Vaughan, Herbert, Crashaw,—saints and sinners all, in their degree, men of flesh and spirit, whose failings we all know from their writings, and read,—recalling, perhaps, Browning's tributes to art and men not wholly blameless, and Blake's proud acceptance of all the universe, good and evil.

Of Donne's poetry Moody himself says, "In moments of illumination, it becomes wonderfully poignant and direct, heart-searching in its simple human accents, with an originality and force for which we look in vain among the clear and fluent melodies of the Elizabethan lyrists." Again the words might be written of Moody's own poetry. We have harmonies and melodies and discords in plenty today; but hardly in any one poet the poignancy, directness, humanity, originality and force that are Moody's.—Of Sir Thomas Browne he says: "His mind was deeply tinged with melancholy, and he shared the prevalent tendency toward religious mysticism. But these qualities are oddly infused with scepticism flowing from his scientific studies, a kind of dreamy, half-credulous scepticism, very different from Bacon's clear-cut rational view of things, but more characteristic of an age in which mediæval and modern ways of thought were still closely mingled together. . . . He loves to stand before the face of the Eternal and the Infinite until the shows of life fade away, and he is filled with a passionate quietude and humility." In Moody mediæval and modern ways of thought are consciously mingled together. In *Good Friday Night* the sceptical modern kneels at last, filled with passionate ecstacy and humility, before the mediæval image of the mother of Christ, his mother, the mother of all. In Moody's letters, too, who does not hear Browne's organ notes reëcho?—No one, again, has written so justly of the spirituality of Fletcher's *Christ Victory and Triumph on Earth and in Heaven*. "The last canto," he says, "which deals with the entrance of Christ into Heaven, is the most beautiful part of the poem. It is a great Easter Hymn, expressing the joy of earthly and heavenly things over the risen Redeemer."

The seventeenth century is famous for the vividness of its conception of Deity. Moody says of Crashaw, "He sings the raptures of the soul visited by divine love, in terms as concrete and glowing as any human lover ever used to celebrate an earthly passion.'' The superhuman but living actuality of the Father and the Son are carried further by Moody. *The Three Angels, The Troubling of the Waters, Jetsam, The Faith Healer,* and the Trilogy disclose fear, hatred, adoration, gratitude, despair,—the gamut of religious feelings. "In Bunyan," says Moody, "we see in its most intense form the religious excitement of the seventeenth century, and also the qualities of imagination which make him so powerful a writer." In Moody, in his turn, we see in words of flame the religious excitement, scepticism and imagination of the nineteenth and twentieth centuries.

Moody nowhere shows his greatness as a poet more than in his treatment of girlhood. In his letters he rhapsodizes over her sheer loveliness as do his friend Stickney, Walter Savage Landor and the young Milton of the Latin Elegies; but in his poetry he strikes out a fine imaginative line like that in *The Fountain*:

"That tawny budding girl, earnest and vague,"

or one all lyrical as in *Heart's Wild-Flower:*

"How blow the shy, shy wilding flowers in the hollows of his wood!"

or adores a real girl with seventeenth century Platonic fervor in *Dawn Parley*. His women, moreover, are triumphant, comparable with Meredith's in power, though more elementally women; women emotionaly or spiritually strong. With knowledge of them profounder even than Donne's, Moody's are the women Donne sings in *The Autumnal,* that eulogy of the noble mother of the Herberts, the warrior and the saint:

Other Essays and Notes

"If 'twere a shame to love, here 'twere no shame,
Affection here takes Reverence's name."

Professor Manly observes that "Moody's poetry was growing into fuller and fuller kinship with that of the elder and most authentic poets of our tongue, while retaining its unmistakable individuality.—Traces of Shakespeare, of Milton, of Keats, of Browning, of Rossetti, of William Morris, of Walt Whitman," continues Professor Manly, "one may find either in theme, or tone, or rhythm, or, though seldom, in phrasal echo." Passion, color, imagination, imagery (sometimes strained), mysticism, melancholy, love of women and religious fervor Moody owed, in part, to the seventeenth century. When we walk in England with Milton, Bunyan, Browne, Walton, Donne, Vaughan, Herbert and Crashaw, Moody walks with us; when we work with Moody in America, or follow the Gleam with him over Europe, the great Englishmen of the seventeenth century accompany us soberly, with strong grave faces.

ADDITIONAL NOTE ON THE SOURCES OF MOODY'S THAMMUZ[32]

I daresay that most readers of William Vaughn Moody's poetry are puzzled by his *Thammuz*. In four stanzas the poet embodies his conception of life as a fusion of religious mysticism and pagan joy. His sources are the Bible, Milton, the myth of Orpheus, and Euripides.

In *On the Morning of Christ's Nativity*, 204, Milton writes,

"In vain the Tyrian maids their Thammuz mourn,"

while at line 460 of *Paradise Lost* he expands *Ezekiel* VIII, 14, as follows:

[32] "The Dial," April 13, 1916.

Other Essays and Notes

> "Thammuz came next behind,
> Whose annual wound in Lebanon allured
> The Syrian damsels to lament his fate
> In amorous ditties all a summer's day,
> While smooth Adonis from his native rock
> Ran purple to the sea, supposed with blood
> Of Thammuz yearly wounded: the love-tale
> Infected Sion's daughters with like heat,
> Whose wanton passions in the sacred porch
> Ezekiel saw, when, by the vision led,
> His eye surveyed the dark idolatries
> Of alienated Judah."

In his edition of *The Complete Poetical Works of John Milton*, Cambridge Edition, 1899, p. 395, Moody has the following note on Milton's Thammuz: "An important figure in Phoenician mythology. He was slain by a boar in Lebanon, but comes to life each spring, his death and resuscitation symbolizing the destructive forces of winter and the quickening forces of spring. When the river Adonis became reddened by the mud brought down from Lebanon by the spring torrents, it was believed to be the flowing afresh of Thammuz's wounds which caused the change of color."

In Moody's *Thammuz* the god is represented as killed by frenzied women. This conception is not innate in the Thammuz-Adonis myth, so Moody effected a combination of the Orpheus story, where love-maddened nymphs slay the hapless singer, with the *Bacchae* of Euripides, in which women crazed by Dionysus tear Pentheus to pieces.

I now venture to quote *Thammuz* entire:

> "Daughters, daughters do ye grieve?
> Crimson dark the freshes flow!
> Were ye violent at eve?
> Crimson stains where the rushes grow!
> What is this that I must know?

"Mourners by the dark red waters,
Met ye Thammuz at his play?
Was your mood upon you, daughters?
Had ye drunken? O how grey
Looks your hair in the rising day!

"Mourners, mourn not overmuch
That ye slew your lovely one.
Such ye are; and be ye such!
Lift your heads; the waters run
Ruby bright in the climbing sun.

"Raven hair and hair of gold,
Look who bendeth over you!
This is not the shepherd old;
This is Thammuz, whom ye slew,
Radiant Thammuz, risen anew!"

VI

William Vaughn Moody and William Blake

OF William Vaughn Moody's Idea of God, Professor Manly says (Introduction to *Poems and Poetic Dramas of William Vaughn Moody,*" p. XLII.): "It was not a formal philosophical conception, but a poetical vision incorporating the most diverse elements of culture." I believe that no one has yet pointed out that the writings of William Blake were one element of that culture. "God figures ambiguously in Moody's poetry," continues Mr. Manly; "sometimes as the Puritan God, whom he does not love and in whom he does not believe; sometimes as the no less anthropomorphic God from whom he cannot keep his fellowship and love."

Now Blake had two Gods also,—the "God of this World," corresponding to Moody's Puritan God, and the Supreme God, whose anthropomorphic nature he set forth in his painting, his lyrics, and his Prophetical Books.

Moody was no such heretic as Blake, yet in his *Masque of Judgment* he "spoke out in meeting," — to use his own words in a letter to Professor Schevill, June 8, 1897. To Mrs. Toy again (Dec. 12, 1900) he writes that the poem is "a plea for passion as a means of salvation everywhere latent." The mythological machinery, he says, "symbolizes the opposed doctrine — that of the denial of life. As Christianity (contrary to the wish and meaning of its founder) has historically linked itself with this doctrine, I included certain aspects of it in this mythological apparatus—always with a semi-satirical intention." Moody's satire and passion here correspond to Blake's war on historical Christianity, and his exaltation of Imagination. Of course they do not include Blake's Everlasting Gospel of Jesus, with its theory of constant and willing forgiveness of all Sin and its identification of Christ and Man with God.

Moody, on the contrary, accepted good and evil in the world, as Blake did; but he did not recommend evil-doing as the first law of Salvation. He wished good and evil to contend with one another, that good might be exercised, and triumph. In Act V of the *Masque of Judgment* Uriel tells Raphael that God "loved not life entirely, good and ill"; adding, "when evil dies, as soon good languishes"; whereupon Raphael, the friend of Man, exclaims:

> "Would he had spared
> That dark Antagonist whose enmity
> Gave Him rejoicing sinews, for of Him,
> His foe was flesh of flesh and bone of bone.
> With suicidal hand He smote him down,
> And now, indeed, His lethal pangs begin."

In *The Brute*, again, the evil that lurks in modern machinery and Efficiency is overpowered in the end by good and serves it. There is no sentimental denial of evil here; nor is there in Blake. But Moody calls on the good to contend with evil. Blake bids the good embrace evil, that Christ may forgive.

Reminiscent of Blake's childhood, when "God put his face to the window" (Moody and Lovett's *History of English Literature*, p. 265) are Moody's lines in Jetsam:

> "Once at a simple turning of the way
> I met God walking."

A passage in Act II (Act IV of the 1909 edition) of the mystical drama, *The Faith Healer,* moreover, recalls Blake's precreation visions. Michaelis says to Rhoda: "Before creation, beyond time, God not yet risen from His sleep, you stand and call to me, and I listen in a dream that I dreamed before Eden." Finally, Moody's *Death of Eve: A Fragment* may owe a suggestion to Blake's *Ghost of Abel*.

Moody writes with enthusiasm of Blake in his *History of English Literature* (pp. 265-6); mentions him in his Letters (autumn, 1895); and refers to him in his edition of Milton (pp. 100-101). "Outwardly Blake led a regular, quiet, laborious life," he says in the first, "all the while pouring out poems, drawings, and vast 'prophetical' books, full of shadowy mythologies and mystical thought-systems, which show that his inward life was one of perhaps unparalleled excitement and adventure. . . . In him the whole transcendental side of the Romantic movement was expressed by hint and implication, though not by accomplishment." "Four-fifths of William Blake would not be accepted for publication by the *Harvard Advocate*," he observes in a humorous letter to Josephine Preston Peabody; with a note of fellow feeling, perhaps, for a romanticist more "floridly extravagant" than his early self. Finally, by way of contrast and correction, he writes as follows in his edition of Milton: "William Blake, in one of his prophetical books, says that Milton's house in the spiritual kingdom is Palladian, not Gothic. Palladian it is, and in this century we have dwelt by preference in the Gothic house of mind, loving the wayward humor of its adornment, the mysticism and confusion of its design. But from time to time we must purify our vision with the more ample and august lines of the house which Milton has builded."

VII

On Moody's Men and Women

WITH what success has Moody characterized men and women? For one thing his studies of women are more searching than those of his men. When he takes for hero an American man he makes of him an unreality like Michaelis in the *Faith Healer* or a miraculously polished diamond like Ghent in *The Great Divide*. These creations embody two aspects of the American desert,—its mysticism and its rough strength and chivalry. Incidentally the two men serve a further purpose: each makes a woman. If God and Man are inseparable to Moody, Woman and Man are not less so. And if his women save his men, in like manner his men save his women. Women saving men is an old theme; men saving women from their new-found rights is a modern note!

To Mr. Herrick the American egoist is not so much the American man as the American woman. Moody was no less earnest, but he had more tolerance, more humor. This comes out in a letter to Daniel Gregory Mason, June 23, 1896. As a Californian I feel a pardonable interest in it. Moody writes:

"I have had an enormous little adventure since I wrote last. Another Girl of course. This time a Westerner *par excellence* — a Californian, dating mentally from the age of Rousseau and Chateaubriand, with geysers and cloudbursts of romanticism, not to say sentimentality; dating spiritually from the Age of Gold, or some remoter purity, some Promethean dawn, some first-foam-birth in hyperborean seas. She likes Gibson's drawings, adores *Munsey's,* and sings 'Don't be Cross, Dear,' with awful unction. After this you will not believe me when I say that she gave me the most unbearable shiver of rapture at the recognition of essential girlhood that I for a long time remember. . . . You can realize the gone feeling that possessed me when she said (interpreting my own gloomy guess) that my kind was not her kind, that my language was not her language, and that her soul could only be studious to avoid mine, as the bird flying southward in spring avoids the hunter. I bowed assent and came home. I now nurse memories and grow elegiac. Come to Chicago!''

In English Literature Moody was attracted by a host of men besides Shakespeare. Milton and the seventeenth century, Blake, Shelley, Keats, Browning, Rossetti, Morris, Arnold and Patmore, at least, influenced his poetry.

His letters, too, disclose the good friends he had among living men; as the minor characters of his two plays, rather than the major, show how successfully he could draw the average American. We need only recall the Newburys and Matthew Beeler. In his poetry he ranges from Raphael, Cain and the spirit of Christ walking with men and women to Old Pourquoi and a soldier fallen in the Philippines. As for his reaction to "the recent notable experience" already quoted, that resulted in *Dawn Parley*, printed by Mr. Mason in the Letters and omitted by Moody in his *Poems*, where he substituted *The Golden Journey*, according to Mrs. Moody. His beautiful *Wilding Flower* was inspired by another girl, a girl who "haunted the symphonies last winter." "What I have tried to say," he wrote to Mr. Mason, "is a thing which constitutes much of the poetry of a young man's life, I think, and if I could have got it said would have had a certain large interpretative value." He did get it said. A third inspiration, whom he calls in another letter to Mason a "compound of ragamuffin, pal, mistress,

Other Essays and Notes

nun, sister, harlequin, outcast and bird of God," plays her large part, as any reader can see by the reappearance of these several types in his composite, generalized poem, *I Am the Woman*.

In addition to these living presences, Moody was fascinated by the character of Eve. In the mother of the race was embodied womanhood dramatically and universally. Besides, Eve had "suffered more than her share of opprobrium at the hands of early Christian and mediæval commentators," as a noted scholar writes.[33]

> "It is I who transgressed the law,
> it is I who committed the transgression,
> it would be right that thou shouldst slay me
> O my Lord, O Adam!"

cries Eve herself in the Celtic *Saltair Na Rann;*[34] while in *Eve's Lament*[35] she takes the blame for the world's woes upon herself in words which I cannot resist quoting in full:

> " 'I am Eve, great Adam's wife,
> 'Tis I that outraged Jesus of old;
> 'Tis I that robbed my children of Heaven,
> By rights 'tis I that should have gone upon the cross.

> " 'I had a kingly house to please me,
> Grievous the evil choice that disgraced me,
> Grievous the wicked advice that withered me!
> Alas! my heart is not pure.

> " ' 'Tis I that plucked the apple,
> Which went across my gullet:

[33] Prof. O. F. Emerson: "Legends of Cain, Especially in Old and Middle English" ("Publications of the Modern Language Association," vol. 21, p. 832, 1906).
[34] Eleanor Hull: "The Poem Book of the Gael," 1912, p. 33.
[35] Kuno Meyer: "Selections from Ancient Irish Poetry," 1911, p. 34.

Other Essays and Notes

So long as they endure in the light of day,
So long will not women cease from folly.

" 'There would be no ice in any place,
There would be no glistening windy winter,
There would be no hell, there would be no sorrow,
There would be no fear, if it were not for me.' "

The third member of Moody's Trilogy is a fragment one act long. *The Death of Eve* had been preceded by an earlier *Death of Eve,* a poem in eleven pages and six parts. The idea in both of these Mr. Lewis[26] finds in Léon Dierx's *La Vision d' Ève,* in thirty elegiac quatrains. But whereas "Dierx boldly made Eve justify the sin of Paradise *before* the crime of Cain, the justification being love,—Moody, still more boldly, designed to justify that sin after Cain's crime, and the justification was to be the whole of life, good and evil together." In her old age Eve seeks Cain to take him before God to tell him she did well. Her assumption of Cain's sin is startling in its intensity. She puts aside the hair from his forehead and cries,

" 'Tis not thy head
Weareth this Sign. 'Tis my most cruel head,
Whose cruel hand, whose swift and bloody hand
Smote in its rage my own fair man-child down.
Not thy hand, Cain, not thine; but my dark hand;
And my dark forehead wears the sign thereof,
As now I take it on me."

Whereupon she kisses him on the Sign.

Moody's chief studies of men, except of men of letters, as we have already noted, are not of marked importance; they are interesting; but they are passing phases. When Ruth Jordan rejects Winthrop because he is "finished, rounded off, a completed product," she is talking that sort

[26] "William Vaughn Moody" ("Yale Review," July, 1913).

of democracy that amuses us in "Western" literature. And a Westerner is particularly skeptical when Ghent is set forth as the typical American. As for Ruth Jordan, when she is read of fifty years from now she may be looked upon as a satire of a stage of American womanhood,—though Moody himself was not satirizing her: he was merely seeing in her the type of girl that preferred Munsey's and the rough, to Winthrop and the finished, and committing her to American letters as she entered the melting-pot, an Eastern girl hand in hand with a Westerner.

But all this is of Moody the dramatist. Moody was not primarily a dramatist, but a poet. As a poet he bids women be women, and men be artists, patriots, reformers, philosophers, men of letters. As a playwright he photographs; as a poet he observes, meditates, digests, universalizes. Even a lyric like *Wilding Flower* has something eternal about it. When he says,

"My sign is set upon her head while stars do meet and sing,"

he speaks finally. The soul of a girl is caught and held fast in the shining net of poetry, his and ours forever. More fittingly, perhaps, I should quote the last stanza of *Dawn Parley,* for there the eternal in the California inspiration of Ruth Jordan is also preserved in verse of "sacred love and sacred art":

"O playmates of her heedless hours
Her eyes ye nevermore may see;
My brain and all my soul's dim powers,
Possess her utterly."

VIII

The Work Of Robert Bridges

With the graphic impressionism of his people, and in their quaint English, Yone Noguchi contributed to the New York *Nation* for October 14th, 1915, an account of a visit to Robert Bridges. Motoring from Oxford to Boar's Head with the poet and his daughter, Mr. Noguchi muses that his children at home will feel proud when they grow older to recall how their father once sat "close as a sardine in a can" to the Laureate. He is well acquainted with Bridges' work and the critics' essays on it. "He has written about what the others forgot when their songs were finished", says he, in Symons' vein. Arrived at Boar's Head, he is hospitably received by Mrs. Bridges. Retiring to his little room, he reads from the Oxford text of Bridges, lulled by the music of the poet's lyrics of Love and Nature. In the morning he awakes to fair English landscape, and after breakfast talks with his host about poetry and prosody. He hears something of Bridges' dislike of publicity and calls him "a chivalrous soul under a rugged exterior." Finally, as they set out on foot towards Oxford, Bridges observes with a smile, "The king knows that I will never do anything foolish."

And that is the note of the latest Laureate, a man whose honors were won wisely, long before he rose to office. In the midst of war he retains his poise. While that other classicist, William Watson, loses control of himself and curses the enemy, Bridges brings out *The Spirit of Man, an Anthology,* a selection of poems to give comfort in time of trouble.

Other Essays and Notes

Robert Bridges was born at Walmer in 1844, of Kentish family. His *Summer House on the Mound* is reminiscent of his boyhood. He was educated at Eton and at Oxford, from which he holds the degrees of M. A., M. B. and Hon. D. Litt. St. Andrews has honored him with its LL.D. After leaving Oxford he traveled, especially in Egypt, Palestine and Italy. He studied medicine in London and practised there, but in 1882 retired to Yattendon, on the downs above Pangbourne, and devoted himself to poetry. Later he removed to Chilswell, Boar's Head, Oxford, where he still lives.

Bridges is an important metrist and authority on English speech. He is impatient of phonetic transcripts, so in his *On the Present State of English Pronunciation*, 1913, he uses fifty-eight type characters: for example, he represents four sounds of *a* by four different forms. In his *Milton's Prosody,* 1893, he discusses stress and syllabic accent in verse. His own *Poems in Classical Prosody* are experiments in fulfillment of a promise to William Johnson Stone (whom see in Professor R. M. Alden's *English Verse*). Stone attempted purely quantitative poetry in English and considered the clash of accent and quantity a beauty rather than a blemish. Bridges does not always agree with Stone as to what constitutes a long syllable; nor that *h* is invariably a consonant (see the Oxford text of Bridges, p. 410). His own prosody is a combination of the stress and syllabic methods; as appears from his *Narcissus:*[27]

>"Almighty wondrous everlasting
>Whether in a cradle of astral whirlfire
>Or globed in a piercing star thou slumb'rest
>   The passionless body of God:
>Thou deep in the core of earth — Almighty! —

[27] Printed in the "Literary Digest," vol. 48, p. 1321 and interpreted in the "Forum," vol. 53, pp. 386-92.

Other Essays and Notes

From numbing stress and gloom profound
Madest escape in life desirous
    To embroider her thin-spun robe.

" 'Twas down in a wood — they tell —
In a running water thou sawest thyself
Or leaning over a pool. The sedges
    Were twinn'd at the mirror's brim;
The sky was there and the trees — Almighty!—
A bird of a bird and white clouds floating
And seeing thou knewest thine own image
And lov'd it beyond all else.

"Then wondering didst thou speak
Of beauty and wisdom of art and worship
Didst build the power of Zeus and Apollo,
    The high cathedrals of Christ.
All that we have is thine — Almighty!—
Heart-felt music and lyric song,
Language, the larger grasp of knowledge,
    All that we think is thine.

"But whence?—Beauteous everlasting!
Whence and whither? Hast thou mistaken
Or dost forget? Look again! Thou seest
    A shadow and not thyself."

Other poems than *Narcissus* not included in the Oxford text may be found by referring to the Readers' Guide to Periodical Literature. For completeness, one may add that in 1895 Bridges published a study of John Keats and in 1911 edited *The Poems of Digby Mackworth Dolben*.

Stephen Phillips, in a note affixed to his *Ulysses*, contrasts his play with Bridges' *Return of Ulysses*, 1890. He shows that Bridges omits Ulysses' adventures prior to his return to Ithaca, whereas *he* retains the Calypso and Hades episodes. William Butler Yeats, on the other hand, eulogizes Bridges and his Ulysses in his *Ideas of Good and Evil*. Yet Bridges' reserve and insistence on unity unquestionably hurt his play, while Phillips' romantic treatment, with its un-Homeric but moving love-scenes with Calypso make an irresistible appeal. It is significant, too, that Phillips' *Nero*, 1906, was anticipated by Bridges' *Nero* (Pt. I, 1885, Pt. II, 1894). Though "lack of vital heat" characterizes Bridges' dramas, there is some warmth and color in *Nero*. However, it remained once more for the stagecraft of Phillips to revivify the theme, and get it declaimed before the footlights, while Bridges' version murmured placidly in the study. In all this, however, it will be seen that Phillips owed almost as much to Bridges for the themes of his plays as to Tennyson for the style of his poetry.

Bridges' other dramas, *The Feast of Bacchus*, 1889, *Achilles in Scyros*, 1890, *The Christian Captives*, 1890, *Palicio*, 1890, and *The Humours of the Court*, 1893, are summarized and discussed by Edward Dowden in his *New Studies in Literature*, 1895, and by F. E. Brett Young in his *Robert Bridges, a Critical Study*, 1914. So is *Prometheus the Firegiver, a Mask in the Greek Manner*, 1883. The *Prometheus* in particular is of interest to Americans to-day, since two successful treatments of the subject have been ours; namely, Trumbull Stickney's and William Vaughn Moody's.

In his and the Lodges' edition of Trumbull Stickney's Poems, Moody acknowledges the indebtedness of his own *Prometheus the Fire-Bringer* to Stickney's *Prometheus Porphyros;* while in his review of Stickney's work in *The North American Review*,[38] he states that "the heroic deed of the Titan brings with it no joy, rather at best only the courage to live and to Deukalion not so much, merely the

[38] vol. 183, p. 1018.

hard necessity. The triumph lies in the deed itself and in the magnanimity which achieved it." This he adds was a natural turn to the story for Stickney, on whom a nameless depression weighed through life.

Though he does not say so, Moody wrote his poem on the same theme to counteract Stickney's quietism, and to set forth his own vigorous conception of the conflict of good and evil. Mr. C. M. Lewis pointed out the good-and-evil theme in Moody in an article in the *Yale Review*, July, 1913. He showed that Moody's Prometheus brings the fire that kindles the elements in torpid man and earth. Mr. Lewis believes further that this turn to the story Moody got and transformed from Leopardi's *History of the Human Race*.

If Moody took anything from Bridges he does not admit it. Bridges' Prometheus is far simpler than Stickney's and Moody's philosophical interpretations. Prometheus is figured forth as one who loves man more than he fears Zeus; who brings man fire unvauntingly, then as modestly retires. The moral of the piece is cheerfully fatalistic: the Fates are above the gods: all is in the hands of the Fates; yet men and gods do not lose courage, nor cease to act.

As a poet, Bridges has been fortunate in his critics, but Edward Dowden's enthusiasm, I think, leads him into an error of judgment when he says that Bridges' *Eros and Pschye* is a better rendering of the Apuleian story than Pater's famous translation in *Marius the Epicurean*. It was not Bridges but Pater who was peculiarly adapted to reproduce the honied sweetness of Apuleius. Before Plato engrossed him, Apuleius was the strongest ancient literary influence on Pater, as we know from *Marius*. Bridges irons out Apuleius; he Hellenizes a Hellenistic African. In his little study of his friend Professor T. Herbert Warren says Bridges was justified because Apuleius is mere tinsel. I "can't see it."

Other Essays and Notes

To find fault a moment longer: Mr. Brett-Young disparages in his Conclusions to his excellent *Robert Bridges: A Critical Study,* such work among the *Later Poems* as *Millicent, Robert Burns: an Epistle on Instinct* and *Ode to Music,* all of which I particularly include in my estimate of the poet as evidences of a somewhat wider range than is commonly attributed to him. *Millicent* has feeling, and comes to one as a pleasant surprise in its stately surroundings. *Robert Burns,* too, is an interesting experiment, made possible by the intellectual poetry of Arnold and Meredith; and the *Ode to Music,* while not powerful, marks Bridges' love of the sister art to poetry, an affection over which Professor Warren makes much in his *Robert Bridges, Poet Laureate,* Oxford, 1913. Indeed, in 1899 Bridges published his *Yattendon Hymnal,* "a most original volume, based," says Professor Warren, "on his own personal experiment and experience with his rustic choir in his parish church on the Berkshire Downs." His friend Henry Ellis Wooldridge wrote the music.

Bridges never rises to the passion of Ernest Dowson's Cynara poem; his realism, when he attempts it in *The Flycatchers* is not nearly so successful as Henley's; and I know no lyric of his quite so lyrical as Lionel Johnson's *To Morfydd.* I mention these four poets together because all have come much under classical influence, ancient and French, though I shall not go into that matter here. Suffice it to say that Bridges can best sustain the classical tone; it seldom fails him. Measure, dignity, restraint, characterize him. *Demeter, A Mask* illustrates these qualities; while the sonnet cycle, *The Growth of Love,* which owes much to Dante, the Shakespeare of the Sonnets, and the youthful Milton, moves forward with stately classic gravity.

In like manner, the *New Poems* and *Later Poems* have

collective and individual excellence: yet no one fails to see at once that Bridges' permanent renown rests on none of these, but on his *Shorter Poems, in Five Books*. They are Latin in their arrangement and in their choiceness. One seems to be reading a Tibullus, with the modern world nicely strained and added. These poems are gem-like things, fair pearls, dew on English lawns,—quests for calm and beauty and love. Bridges must always appeal to those who admire him as a minor Wordsworth; a poet exquisitely attuned to the gentler notes of Nature; a poet at peace with Earth and Man.

"I love all beauteous things,
 I seek and adore them,"

he sings; and

"I too will something make
And joy in the making."

He *has* in *The Cliff-Top*. Listen and behold:

"The cliff-top has a carpet
 Of lilac, gold and green:
The blue sky bounds the ocean,
 The white clouds scud between.

A flock of gulls are wheeling
 And wailing round my seat;
Above my head the heaven,
 The sea beneath my feet."

But

"When winds without make moan,
I love my own fireside
Not least when most alone.

Then oft I turn the page
In which our country's name,

Spoiling the Greek of fame,
Shall sound in every age.

Or some Terentian play
Renew, whose excellent
Adjusted folds betray
How once Menander went."

Where begin, where end quoting him? Here is his warning to cynics:

"Earth hath no sin but thine,
Dull eyes of scorn:
O'er thee the sun doth pine
And angels mourn."

Here speaks the man at peace:

"And every eve I say,
Noting my step in bliss,
That I have known no day
In all my life like this."

IX
Alas, Poor Yorick!

"RIGHT GLAD I AM," says Tristam Shandy, in Chapter IV of the first Book of his Life and Opinions, "That I have begun the history of myself in the way I have done; and that I am able to go on, tracing everything in it, as Horace says, *ab ovo*.

"*Horace*, I know, does not recommend this fashion altogether: But that gentleman is speaking only of an epic poem, or a tragedy;— (I forget which) — besides, if it was not so, I should beg Mr. Horace's pardon;—for in writing what I have set about, I shall confine myself neither to his rules, nor to any man's rules that ever lived." "And in this, Sir", he concludes his first Book, "I am of so nice and singular a humour, that if I thought you was able to form the least judgment or probable conjecture to your self, of what was to come in the next page,—I would tear it out of my book".

The erudition of *Tristam Shandy* edified Sterne's fashionable readers; but in 1798 Dr. Ferriar showed in his *Illustrations* that portions of it were appropriated from Rabelais and Burton; with suggestions from Bruscambille, Beroalde de Verville, Bouchet, Scarron, Swift, "Gabriel John", Blount, Bacon, Montaigne and Bishop Hall. Isaac D'Israeli added John Dunton's *Voyage Round the World*. Sterne concealed his sources (except Cervantes) with astonishing care, considering his frankness in all else: Cross calls it his master stroke of humor. But perhaps he also enjoyed his reputation for learning. He appeared to know everything; he adduced authorities ancient, mediæval and modern; he incorporated them into his droll book; he reached cynics, courtiers and ladies unequipped with the higher education. Like many modern teachers he taught by successfully amusing,[39] and died of making people laugh and learn. To illustrate: in the twentieth chapter of Book I he requests his fair reader to peruse the last chapter again, because she has skipped the allusions. " 'Tis to rebuke a vicious taste," he continues, "which has crept into thousands besides herself,—of reading straight forwards, more in quest of the adventure than of the deep erudition and knowledge which a book of this cast, if read over as it should be, would infallibly impart with them. The mind should be accustomed to make wise reflections, and draw curious conclusions as it goes along; the habitude of which made *Pliny* the younger affirm, 'That he never read a book so bad, but he drew some profit from it.' The stories of *Greece* and *Rome,* run over without this turn and application,—do less service, I affirm it, than the history of *Parismus* and *Parismenus,* or of the Seven Champions of *England,* read with it." This is humorous; but who shall say it did not influence Sterne's readers, who hung breathless on his words, to read the learned passages at least once, to marvel at Yorick's knowledge and to absorb a little themselves? On the other hand, in Book IV, chapter XXII, he declares that if his book is "wrote" against anything,— " 'tis wrote, an' please your worships, against the spleen!" And his dedication of the second edition, April, 1860, To the Right Honourable Mr. Pitt reads, "If I am ever told it has made you smile; or can conceive it has beguiled you

---

[39] E. Hermann: "Eucken and Bergson," p. 47, speaks of "that 'esprit' and that almost journalistic lightness and impressionism of touch which the modern epicure of mind expects even from the gravest teacher." Sterne is, indeed, England's greatest prose impressionist (see Ivor Campbell on Sterne in the "Oxford and Cambridge Review," IX, p. 97).

Other Essays and Notes

of one moment's pain — I shall think myself as happy as a minister of state.''

Neither Cross nor Leslie Stephen see anything but the artist (quite enough, most say) in Sterne: he lacked moral sense; he pursued sensations for their own sake; he was a slave to his humors. We doubt, though, for our part, that his writing, his preaching, his learning, his epicureanism, and his gospel of mirth were all a jest to Sterne, Yorick though he was. For the King's Jester sets the king laughing and thinking; thinking that pomposity and pose are ridiculous, and recalling that a good man, like Uncle Toby, is the salt of the earth. The moralists have pierced Sterne with an epithet; he is a sentimentalist; yet there is a genuine strain of tenderness in him that was salutary for the eighteenth century. Thackeray (*Sterne and Goldsmith*) speaks of his foul Satyr's eyes leering constantly out of the leaves; yet he grants that ''all his letters to his daughter are artless, kind, affectionate and not sentimental; as a hundred pages in his writings are beautiful and full, not of surprising humour merely, but of genuine love and kindness.''[40]

In Book I, chapter XI of *Tristam Shandy*, Sterne writes a defence of himself. ''Yorick,'' he says, ''had an invincible dislike and opposition in his nature to gravity;— not to gravity as such;—for where gravity was wanted, he would be the most grave and serious of mortal men for days and weeks together; but he was an enemy to the affectation of it, and declared open war against it, only as it appeared a cloak for ignorance or for folly; and then, whenever it fell in his way, however sheltered and protected,

---

[40] Ivor Campbell in ''Laurence Sterne'' (''Oxford and Cambridge Review,'' IX, p. 105) says of ''Tristam Shandy,'' ''There is a magical fragrance of kindness, a large humanity about this book which leaves one very contented with life.''

he seldom gave it much quarter. . . . In the naked temper which a merry heart discovered, he would say there was no danger,—but to itself:— whereas the very essence of gravity was design, and consequently deceit;—'twas a taught trick to gain credit of the world for more sense and knowledge than a man was worth".

In a letter written on November 16, 1764 to Mr. Foley at Paris, he takes Shandeism quite seriously. "We must be happy within," he says, "and then few things without us make much difference — This is my Shandean philosophy." It is also the Epicurean or even the Stoic doctrine of the unruffled mind. Further evidence of his Epicureanism is pointed out by Mr. Sichel:[41] "Through all his variations one element reigns,—an insouciance that sports with trouble, extracting the sweet from the bitter. 'Great Apollo', he exclaims, 'if thou art in a good humour, give me, I ask no more, but one stroke of native humour with a single spark of thy power along with it, and send Mercury with the rules and compasses, if he can be spared, with my compliments — no matter.' The rules and compasses he scorned, and his was a pagan resignation,—the philosophy of which Goethe approved." Like Horace, he was a Stoic and an Epicurean by turns. He drew such pleasure from the world as it afforded him, and endured what he could not change. Besides, he wrested from its context in the *Ars Poetica* (where it is not sentimental) Horace's precept for tragedy

"Si vis me flere, dolendum est
Primum ipsi tibi; tunc tua me infortunia laedent,"[42]

and was constantly being moved to tears himself that he might move others.

[41] "Sterne, A Study," 1910.
[42] "If you would have me weep, you must first suffer yourself; then your misfortunes will give me pain."

Other Essays and Notes

We have probably given too much space (that hackneyed exercise whenever comedy and satire are mentioned) to showing that a strain of the serious exists in this great wit and humorist, but condemnation of Sterne has been severe. Hawthorne, on the other hand, said of Sterne that the world has treated with singular harshness a writer who has done so much for it.[43] So much so, indeed, that Professor Saintsbury in the *Bookman*[44] swings to the far side, admitting all that is said against Sterne, and asking what, in the end, are the odds? a characteristic twentieth century tolerant solution of difficulties. After all, he declares, there was no bad blood in him, and as an artist his uniqueness is unquestioned. Who has equalled, who can imitate his *Sentimental Journey?* Who, after all, denies Sterne genius? Who, we may add in another strain,—we Americans who worship Success,—who, knowing Sterne's childhood and his weak body, will deny that he succeeded in literature if not in life, leaving a name to conjure with?

[43] "Our Old Home: Pilgrimage to Old Boston."
[44] "The Living Age," vol. 278, pp. 480-84, Aug. 23, 1913.

X
In Praise of Euphranor

IN the *Variorum and Definitive Edition of the Poetical and Prose Writings of Edward FitzGerald,* 1902, vol. I, p. xxv, Mr. Gosse writes, "What FitzGerald could do in prose we know from his correspondence and from 'Euphranor.' It has stately passages, and the final page no doubt deserves the high commendation of Tennyson; it possessed to the Cambridge men the charm of recalling with delicate local colour the dialectics of their youth, but when all is said and done it remains a little lifeless and unrealized, a little uninteresting, to tell the blunt truth. In its form and setting, it seems to follow the 'Alciphron' of Berkeley, but at how great a distance!" Turning to Mr. Gosse's *History of Eighteenth Century Literature,* p. 201, we read of *Alciphron:* "This is the longest of Berkeley's books, and perhaps the most easy for the outsider to understand; philosophers have condemned it as the least valuable. The scene of the book is laid in Rhode Island, and the form is that of the Platonic dialogue, in its most polished and graceful shape. The dialogues are seven, and there is a slight setting of landscape to each, with a hint of woods and gardens, and the distant hallo of the fox-hunter."

Alciphron and *Euphranor,* then, appeal to Mr. Gosse rather on their literary than on their philosophical sides. As a work of art, and as an example of Platonic imitation, he places *Alchiphron* far above *Euphranor.*

That the professional idealist philosopher Berkeley approached the form of the Platonic dialogue more nearly than the dreamy Epicurean FitzGerald is indisputable; that he caught the poetical spirit of Plato's lighter moments as subtly as did FitzGerald is as unquestioned. He did not. "Taste is the feminine of genius," said FitzGerald many times. So fine was his taste that he could criticize his own works as keenly as another's (more so, if we accept George Meredith's observations in a letter to Edward Clodd, September 16, 1898: "His taste in the Classics is quite sound, and infantile out of them!"). FitzGerald himself approved of *Euphranor,* which he called "a pretty specimen of 'Chisell'd Cherry-Stone,' " (Letter to Charles Eliot Norton, June 9, 1882). Yet he admitted (Letter to Cowell, 1845) the difficulty of keeping up "the good dialectic," and yet maintaining "the disjected sway of natural conversation;" in short, the difficulty of conversing at once like Plato and FitzGerald. That he succeeded in making his English boys both beautifully Greek and charmingly English is a triumph of no mean order; a triumph to which *Alciphron,* with all its merits, does not attain. For who will say that Berkeley's philosophers have the Platonic artistry of speech, keeping up the good dialectic and yet maintaining the disjected sway of natural conversation? Are they not, to the end, too obviously mouthpieces of Berkeley, Shaftesbury, Mandeville and others? FitzGerald's boys, on the contrary, do not talk FitzGerald, or, as we more commonly say, Omar. Every word they utter is in character; they cannot even be charged, as Plato's Socrates can so often, with talking Plato. They talk "in shape of dialogue really something Platonic," to quote from FitzGerald's letter to Cowell, May 28, 1868: a phrase of FitzGerald's own perfect characterization. Once, says he, to Cowell, 1847, "the spirit of light dialogue evaporated from me during an influenza. . . . I do not think I can have much personal ambition in its success; but I should sincerely wish it to be read for what little benefit it may do (To G. Crabbe, Feb. 11, 1851). . . . I remember being anxious about it twenty years ago, because I thought it was the Truth (as if my telling it could mend the matter!): and I cannot but think the Generation that has grown up in these twenty years has not profited by the Fifty Thousand copies of this great work!'' (To Cowell, 1868). So runs the current of his thoughts.

For myself, first and last, after reading *Euphranor* in different years and places, I continue to get the same sense of perfect art from it. "What genuine student of literature would exchange for a wilderness of abstract categories the letters in which FitzGerald communicates the thrill of his literary admirations?" asks Professor Shorey. Nay, who would exchange FitzGerald's *Euphranor* for Berkeley's *Alciphron?* Happily, we have both,—*Alciphron* for Mr. Gosse, *Euphranor* for FitzGerald's many admirers; among whom Mr. Gosse is in most respects among the foremost.

XI
Walter Savage Landor, Eliza Lynn Linton and Julia Landor

THE *Yale Review* for January, 1916, contains an essay on *Swinburne and Carducci* that is above reproach, except for two strange errors. One is the common mistake of calling Swinburne a classicist, whereas, though a Grecian, no one was more a romanticist than he. The other is perhaps the more pardonable one — except among "specialists" — of referring to Mrs. Lynn Lyndon (the name should be Lynn Linton) as the daughter of Walter Savage Landor.

Swinburne prefaced his *Song for the Centenary of Walter Savage Landor* (*Studies in Song*, 1880) with a *Dedication to Mrs. Lynn Linton*. The first half of the poem reads:

> "Daughter in spirit elect and consecrate
>   By love and reverence of the Olympian sire
> Whom I too loved and worshipped, seeing so great,
>   And found so gracious toward my long desire
> To bid that love in song before his gate
>   Sound, and my lute be loyal to his lyre.
> To none save one it now may dedicate
>   Song's new burnt-offering on a century's pyre."

Mrs. Lynn Linton, then, was only daughter in spirit to Swinburne's Olympian sire.

The eulogy of Landor that undoubtedly called forth Swinburne's panegyric, namely E. Lynn Linton's *Reminiscences of Walter Savage Landor* in *Fraser's Magazine* for 1870, is one of the triumphs of appreciation in English.

I can only think of Colvin on Stevenson, Symons on Dowson, or the early Le Gallienne on Meredith to compare with it. So ardent a defence of the passionate old man deserves wide reading, and excuses quotation. "For twelve years Mr. Landor held with me the place of a father," says she, "ever indulgent, kind and generous, I being at all times like his loving and dutiful child. Hence I am better qualified to speak of him personally than any other of his literary friends." And later, "I stayed with him long and often, and I never had one moment's coolness with him; never the faintest shadow of misunderstanding or displeasure. I was afraid of him, granted; as was befitting in one standing in the relation of daughter to a father so infinitely superior to herself. I loved him then, and I love his memory now, as that of a dear and honoured father, and I am not ashamed to confess my awe and fear." And again, "For twelve, long, dear years, we were father and daughter; we never called each other anything else; he never signed himself to me, or wrote to me, as anything else; and in the last sad clouded days of his life, had not the circumstances of my own life been so changed as to render it impossible, I would have gone with him to Italy, and I would not have left him again while he lived."

That Landor was signally appreciative of the devotion of his foster-daughter appears from Forster's statement that Landor replaced a dedication to his *Last Fruit Off an Old Tree* to that strange man of genius whom Landor admired and Forster disliked,—Thomas Lovell Beddoes—by one to Mrs. Lynn Linton. Stephen Wheeler, again, notes in his *Letters and Unpublished Writings of Walter Savage Landor* that Landor wished a copy of his *Letters of a Canadian* sent to Monckton Milnes, Kenneth Mackenzie and Mrs. Linton. Verses to her as the author of *Amymone, a*

Other Essays and Notes

Romance of the Days of Pericles, were published by Landor in the *Examiner* of July 22, 1848.[45] Finally, in a letter to Mrs. Graves-Sawle[45] he says of the "good Luisina," granddaughter of "Ianthe," and of Eliza Lynn, who came to see him on Saturday, "What a charm it is even at the close of life to be cared for by the beautiful and gentle, and to see them come ~~and~~ out from the warm sunshine and the sweet flowers toward us in the chilliness of our resting place. This is charity, the charity of the Graces."

From such passages, the student of *Mrs. Lynn Linton, Her Life Letters and Opinions*, as George Somes Layard calls his book about her, sees that as the foremost opponent of the cruder aspects of Women's Rights, Mrs. Linton, with her ideal of the "old-fashioned girl" practiced the devotion she preached. Meredith criticized her books as "very sour in tendency, hard in style, forced, and exemplifying the author's abhorrence of the emancipation of young females from their ancient rule."[46] Yet her *Girl of the Period*, in the *Saturday Review* of March 14, 1868, is almost as fair a reading of the Sex from one point of view in her day and ours as Meredith's more searching analyses from another. In her married life, unluckily for her theories, Mrs. Linton was unhappy; but her heart continued to go out with undiminished affection to Landor. She not only watched over him with jealous care while he lived, but she took Forster's Life of him to task when he was dead. "With all his passion, ferocity and coarseness when roused" she wrote in the *North British Review* of 1869, "there was an amount of purity of feeling in him unequalled, and a capacity for the most refined and idyllic tenderness as great as was his ca-

---

[45] Stephen Wheeler: "Letters of Walter Savage Landor, Private and Public," p. 173.
[46] B. W. Matz: "George Meredith as Publisher's Reader," ("Fortnightly Review," N. S., vol. 86, p. 286).

pacity for anger, pride and hatred. Mr. Forster makes but little account of this."

Finally, we should not forget that in addition to the fatherly regard he felt for Rose Paynter, Miss Kate Field and Eliza Lynn Linton, Landor had a daughter of his own, Julia Elizabeth Savage Landor. His references to her in his letters to Rose Paynter are wistful and affectionate. After his separation from his wife he saw little of his children. In 1843, however, Julia and her brother Walter were to visit him at Bath. In expectation of their coming Landor wrote to his daughter the lines that appeared in *Blackwood's Magazine*, March 1843:

"By that dejected city, Arno runs,
Where Ugolino claspt his famisht sons.
There wert thou born, my Julia! there thine eyes
Return'd as bright a blue to vernal skies.
And thence, my little wanderer! when the Spring
Advanced, thee, too, the Hours on silent wing
Brought, while anemonies were quivering round,
And pointed tulips pierced the purple ground,
Where stood fair Florence: there thy voice first blest
My ear, and sank like balm into my breast:
For many griefs had wounded it, and more
Thy little hands could lighten were in store.
But why revert to griefs? Thy sculptur'd brow
Dispels from mine its darkest cloud even now.
What then the bliss to see again thy face,
And all that Rumour has announced of grace!
I urge, with fevered breast, the four-month day.
O! could I sleep to wake again in May.

His Julia came, and he put the thought of losing her again from him. But she had promised to be away only six months. "My Julia went by the steamer on Sunday," he wrote to Rose Paynter in 1843. "The weather was very boisterous. I rose several times in the night and attempted by putting my hand out of the window to ascertain in which point was the wind. . . . My dear Julia wished not only to be with me, but alone with me as much as possible. We parted in unutterable grief, but youth and fresh scenes will soon assuage all hers. That is enough.

"Adieu, dear Rose."

XII

The Influence of Nonnus on Elizabeth Barrett Browning, Thomas Love Peacock and Walter Pater

PROFESSOR LEWIS P. CHAMBERLAYNE'S *A Study of Nonnus* (*Studies in Philology*, Bain Memorial Number, *The University of North Carolina*, Jan., 1916, pp. 40-68) should be inserted in every student's history of Greek Literature. A note may be added, however, on Nonnus's influence on Mrs. Browning, Thomas Love Peacock and Walter Pater. One of these, namely Peacock, knew Nonnus well.

On August 16, 1851, "Aegrotus" wrote to *Notes and Queries*, "I shall be obliged if any of your correspondents will inform me if any translation of the poet Nonnus, which contains perhaps, most that is known about Bacchus, has ever been made into English; and if so, by whom?"

I do not know that Aegrotus received a favorable reply; though Nonnus *had* been translated in part by "Vida" in *The London Magazine* in 1822.

Moreover just six years before his letter, on August 20, 1845, Elizabeth Barrett Browning wrote to Robert Browning, "Did I not tell you that early in the summer I did some translation for Miss Thomson's 'Classical Album', from Bion and Theocritus, and Nonnus, the author of that large (not great) poem in some forty books of the 'Dionysiaca' . . . and the paraphrases from Apuleius? Well— I had a letter from her the other day, full of compunction and ejaculations, and declaring the fact that Mr. Burges had been correcting all the proofs of the poems, leaving out and emending generally, according to his own particular idea of the pattern in the mount — is it not amusing? I have been wicked enough to write in reply that it is happy for her and all readers—*sua si bona norint*—if during some half hour which otherwise might have been dedicated by Mr. Burges to putting out the lights of Sophocles and his peers, he was satisfied with the humbler devastations of E. B. B. upon Nonnus. You know it is impossible to help being amused. This correcting is a mania with that man! And then I, who wrote what I did from the 'Dionysiaca,' with no respect for 'any author', and an arbitrary will to 'put the case' of Bacchus and Ariadne as well as I could, for the sake of the art-illustrations,—those subjects Miss Thomson sent me,—and did it all with full liberty and persuasion of soul that nobody would think it worth while to compare English with Greek and refer me back to Nonnus and detect my wanderings from the text!! But the critic was not to be cheated so! And I do not doubt that he has set me all 'to rights' from beginning to end; and combed Ariadne's hair close to her cheeks for me. Have *you* known Nonnus,—you who forget nothing? and have known everything, I think?"

Browning evidently had *not* known Nonnus; at least he begs the question in his reply by turning upon Burges, over whose scholarship and "discoveries" he makes merry. As a result, as far as I can find out, these translations intended for Miss Thomson were not published by her; they seem to have appeared first in Mrs. Browning's *Last Poems*, 1862. At any rate as they stand to-day in any complete edition of her works they are entitled *From Nonnus: How Bacchus Finds Ariadne Sleeping,* and *How Bacchus Com-*

Other Essays and Notes

forts Ariadne,—both from the *Dionysiaca,* Book XLVII, and amounting to one hundred and thirty lines.

But Mrs. Browning's knowledge of Nonnus was slight compared with that of Thomas Love Peacock. "Peacock," says Oliver Elton in his *Survey of English Literature,* 1780-1830, I, 379, "is fond of the poets, like Nonnus, of the decadence." "He had a distinct weakness for Nonnus, whose *Dionysiaca* he asserted was the finest poem in the world after the *Iliad* (*Calidore,* etc., p. 20)," says Dr. Carl Van Doren in his scholarly *Life of Thomas Love Peacock,* pp. 18-19, "and he used to take a malicious pleasure in finding Oxford scholars who knew not the Panopolitan." In his famous *The Four Ages of Poetry* — iron, or bardic, golden, or Homeric, silver, or Virgilian, and brass, or Nonnic,— Peacock writes of the brass age: "The best specimen of it, though not the most generally known, is the *Dionysiaca* of Nonnus, which contains many passages of exceeding beauty in the midst of masses of amplification and repetition." Writing to Shelley, Aug. 19, 1818 (see Van Doren, p. 134) he says. "I read Nonnus occasionally. The twelfth book, which contains the 'Metamorphosis of Ampelus', is very beautiful, and concludes with an animated picture of the dance of the inebriated Satyrs when Bacchus made his first wine-press, by digging a hole in a rock, and horn (afterwards sacred in consequence) was used instead of cups." Peacock quotes from Nonnus in *Crotchet Castle,* Chapters II and XIV, and in *The Misfortunes of Elphin,* Chapters III, VIII and X.

In 1816-18 Peacock projected a poem on nympholepsy, with Nonnus as one of his sources, but did not complete it (Van Doren, p. 110). Finally, his enthusiasm for Nonnus was so well known that when an anonymous writer contributed an article *On the Poetry of Nonnus,* with considerable

Other Essays and Notes

translations from the *Dionysiaca* to *The London Magazine* for October and November, 1822, several persons, then and since, thought that Peacock was the author of it. (Van Doren, 155-6).

Unlike Andrew Lang, who does not cite Nonnus in his *Myth, Ritual and Religion*, Walter Pater mentions him near the end of his *A Study of Dionysus* (*Greek Studies*). He says the "Orphic poem, *The Occultations of Dionysus*, is represented only by the details that have passed from it into the almost endless *Dionysiaca* of Nonnus, a writer of the fourth century." Whether or not at the suggestion of this passage, J. G. Frazer, in his *Spirits of the Corn and of the Wild*, 1912, vol. I, ch. I, pp. 12-13, *Dionysus*, gives the substance of the *Dionysiaca*, *VI*, 155-205, regarding the birth and destruction of the god. Pater's knowledge of Nonnus was probably not much more extensive than Mrs. Browning's or Frazer's; certainly it did not equal Peacock's.

XIII
A Minor Note in Arthur Symons

Lionel Johnson declared that as a poet Symons was a slave to impressionism; yet how admirably that slavery serves him in his *Cities*, or in his little *Search in Spain!* And deserting impressionism now and then, how pregnant a sentence he can utter, as when he writes in *Venice*, "A realist, in Venice, would become a romantic, by mere faithfulness to what he saw before him;" or in *Naples*, "At Easter the Neapolitans mourn for Jesus Christ as the Greeks mourned for the death of Adonis." And how like the balm of Greek and Roman letters upon the modern spirit is the silence of the city Rome on him, giving peace to his soul, delivering him at once "from the tyranny of the senses and the ideas of pure reason."

Classicism is but a minor note in Symons, but the ancient tradition, which comes to him usually with a romantic and realistic turn through France, has not lived in vain when it can induce so marked a romanticist to recognize the fine quality of Landor and to acknowledge with enthusiasm that Robert Bridges' poise, temperance and self-control are as important to poetry and life as "passions more vehement, thoughts more profound, wilder music, more variable colour." He is attracted to what he calls Bridges' calm rapture. "Here," he writes, "is an artist so scrupulous that beauty itself must come only in sober apparel, joy walking temperately, sorrow without the private disfigurement of tears." And Landor appeals to him so far that he includes in his *Romantic Movement in*

English Poetry a writer primarily a classicist. "His verse," says he, "has at its best an austere nobility, a delicate sensitiveness, the quantities of marble or of onyx"; while "every phrase (of his prose) comes to us with the composure and the solemnity of verse but with an easier carriage under restraint."

Such appreciation of classicists may fittingly be placed beside Symons' thrilling essay on Ernest Dowson, or that perfect characterization and interpretation, *Pachmann at the Piano (Plays, Acting and Music)*: studies in which he rises to Pater's conception of great criticism, making of it a fine art.

XIV

The Major Note in Thomas Hardy

WRITING in *Pa*t*rins*, 1892, of *Wilful Sadness in Literature* Miss Louise Imogene Guiney observes that "some public censor, a Stoic having a heart, and perfect control of it, should be appointed, in every township, to kill off what is uselessly doleful, in the egg, and spread abroad the right idea of what is fit to be uttered in this valley of tears. . . . Mr. Meredith's influence, in our own day, is not such as will induce you to sit shaking your maudlin head over yourself and all creation; neither need it be added? is Mr. Stevenson's."

As far as novels go, the present writer is a Meredithian by progression from a Stevensonian, but for the life of him he cannot evolve further into a Hardyan. On the contrary, he was inspired, until he read S. Law Wilson on *The Theology of Thomas Hardy*, to apply Miss Guiney's words to the great recreator of Wessex; and if too late to help kill in the egg, at least to mourn audibly with Meredith "Hardy's twilight view of life." But Mr. Wilson has done this, and more, with evangelical fervor. Yet a Californian, born to sunlight, cannot but agree with Lionel Johnson's gentle critic that wilful gloom in literature is a sad thing; nor help regretting that Hardy does not oftener leave Wessex peasants to dwell with Meredith's ladies of the future and men of birth or breeding, or come up to London, when "blue", to his Club,—to see the lights and overlook the fog.

To disassociate Hardy and Meredith, even when one is not contrasting the Pessimism of the one with the Opti-

Other Essays and Notes

mism of the other, or the sensibility of the one with the sense of the other; or the humble folk of the one with the gentlefolk of the other, is out of the question, but can be abbreviated. Meredith read Hardy's first novel for Chapman and Hall and criticized its want of plot; then, after much good advice (which he did not follow himself, according to Mr. Hardy) so encouraged the new novelist that *Desperate Remedies* was written and published. Hardy always looked up to the great Reader, and when Meredith died addressed a poem to *G. M., 1828-1909.* In it he said

> "Forty years back, when much had place
> That since has perished out of mind,
> I heard that voice, and saw that face.
>
> "He spoke as one afoot will wind
> A morning horn ere men awake;
> His note was trenchant, smart, but kind.
>
> "He was of those whose words can shake
> And riddle to the very core
> The falsities that Time will break." . . .

"So why laugh at them?" he seems to add. "Pity them; they are foreordered; the years dissolve them." But he checks himself and continues

> "Of late when we two met once more,
> The luminous countenance and rare
> Shone just as forty years before.
>
> "So that, when now all tongues declare
> He is unseen by his green hill,
> I scarce believe he sits not there.
>
> "No matter. Further and further still
> Through the world's vaporous vitiate air
> His words wing on — as strong words will."

Other Essays and Notes

Unlike William Vaughn Moody in *The Daguerreotype* Hardy does not discuss himself while yet unborn; but he pities the unborn generally. He finds them

> "Driven forward like a rabble rout
> Into the world they had so desired
> By the all-immanent Will."

He sings himself and his mother cheerfully enough, however, in *The Roman Road*.

> "The Roman Road runs straight and bare
> As the pale parting-line in hair
> Across the heath. And thoughtful men
> Contrast its days of Now and Then,
> And delve and measure and compare;
>
> "Visioning on the vacant air
> Helmed legionaries, who proudly rear
> The Eagle, as they pace again
>   The Roman Road.
>
> "But no tall brass-helmed legionnaire
> Haunts it for me. Uprises there
> A mother's form upon my ken,
> Guiding my infant steps as when
> We walked that ancient thoroughfare,
>   The Roman Road.

"Hardy himself began to undergo life in 1840," a critic has said wittily. He was born near Dorchester, and still lives there. "I shall keep a school as near to Egdon as possible, so as to be able to walk over and have a night-school in my mother's house," says Clym Yeobright in *The Return of the Native*. Hardy has kept his school for many years by Egdon Heath and the nights and the days have grown steadily darker. His pupils — the peasant poor of Wessex — do not emigrate. They stay at home enduring.

Other Essays and Notes

Only the brighter, hardier spirits go into cities, or come to America. For himself, Hardy sends his regrets in verse to *An Invitation to the United States*. He says,

> "My ardours for high emprise lost
> Since life has bared its bones to me,
> I shrink to seek a modern coast
> Whose riper times have yet to be;
> From that long drip of human tears
> Which people old in tragedy
> Have left upon the centuried years.
> For wonning in these ancient lands,
> Enchased and lettered as a tomb,
> And scored with prints of perished hands,
> And chronicled with dates of doom,
> Though my own Being bear no bloom
> I trace the lives such scenes enshrine,
> Give past exemplars present room,
> And their experience count as mine."

He receives visitors kindly, however, and one is pleased to learn from Professor Alden that England's great pessimist is eminently cheerful as a host. In this connection *An August Midnight* discloses him welcoming callers humbler but wiser:

> "A shaded lamp and a waving blind,
> And the beat of a clock from a distant floor:
> On this scene enter — winged, bowed and spined —
> A longlegs, a moth, and a dumbledore;
> While 'mid my page there idly stands
> A sleepy fly, that rubs its hands. . . .
>
> "Thus meet we five in this still place,
> At this point of time, at this point in space.
> — My guests parade my new-penned ink,
> Or bang at the lamp-glass, whirl and sink.
> 'God's humblest, they!' I muse. Yet why?
> They know Earth-secrets that know not I."

Other Essays and Notes

In *In a Wood* Hardy evidently left the Town, the House and the gloomy Heath long enough to take Meredith's advice, "When in trouble, go out and talk to nature." He was doomed to disillusionment. For when he got among the trees he found them shouldering and elbowing one another with all the envy and malice of men:

> "Since then no grace I find
>   Taught me of trees
> Turn I back to my kind,
>   Worthy as these.
> There at least smiles abound,
> There discourse trills around,
> There, now and then, are found
>   Life loyalties."

Indeed, in his personal relations, Hardy seems an exception to the rule of the *genus irritabile*. "Truth will be truth always," he obseres in his *To a Lady Offended by a Book of the Writer's;* and bids her dreams of him and his
   "Yield their space to shine of smugger things."
But in general he is not called upon to chide *persons,* who are all creatures of Fate, or mourn material ill-fortune of his own. England has honored him with the Order of Merit, Dorchester has bestowed on him the Freedom of the Town and Cambridge and Aberdeen have conferred honorary degrees on him. The War has caused his *Dynasts* to be produced on the stage, for which, as a closet-drama, it was not intended. Hardy's quarrel is not with man, but with the Will and Nature. However, he wonders himself, at times, whether he ought to divulge all he knows. He asks in *The Problem*:

> "Shall we conceal the case, or tell it —
>   We who believe the evidence?
> Here and there the watch-towers knell it,

Other Essays and Notes

> With a sullen significance,
> Heard of the few who hearken intently
> And carry an eagerly upstrained sense
> Hearts that are happiest hold not by it;
> Better we let, then, the old view reign;
> Since there is peace in it, why decry it?
> Since there is comfort, why disdain?
> Note not the pigment the while that the painting
> Determines humanity's joy and pain."

Whatever the attitude of the three great Greek tragedians may have been towards the gods — and how can we say finally, with so many of their plays lost?—Hardy has passed Euripides by and drawn two pagan conceptions for his sad uses, one from Sophocles, the other from Aeschylus. In Sophocles he finds the idea of Fate, accepts it, deplores it, and preaches resignation to it. From Aeschylus he gets Promethean revolt, studies its workings in peasants and kings, mourns its futility, and discloses its victims overtaken by destruction.

"Neither Hardy nor Sophocles has formulated a theory of causation," says Benjamin de Casseres.[47] "A blind, omnipotent, non-moral force sways the affairs of men." In *For Conscience Sake (Life's Little Ironies)* both Millborne and Antigone observe an honorable rite, only to obtain for themselves "the reward of dishonorable laxity." In *The Dynasts*, First Volume, Fifth Act, Fourth Scene, the Spirit of the Pities quotes the *Trachiniae*, 1266-72; where Sophocles, says Pity, dubbs the Will the gods, who cover men with mournfulness, themselves with shame.

In Chapter I of *The Woodlanders* Hardy sets forth his theory that in sequestered spots "dramas of a grandeur and unity truly Sophoclean are enacted in the real." His great-

[47] "Thomas Hardy's Women" ("Bookman," vol. 16).

er novels and the *Dynasts* are attempts to apply the principles of Greek tragedy to humble life in Wessex and to the epic events of the Napoleonic wars. But it is only to the latter that they are fittingly and successfully adapted. Greek tragedy is exalted, a matter of gods and heroic men and women. The simple folk of Wessex are not Titanic, not alone because of humble birth, but from want of conscious warring with Fate. Their misfortunes do not come of their own sins and follies, or those of their families or race, but from the blind working of the Will. Tess, Jude and Eustacia are not defiers of the gods. True, they are "above their station" and long for better things. To show that such aspiration is folly, with the Will what it is, and to quench these soaring souls, gives content to Hardy's fatalism. If Hardy blamed men unmistakably for their own faults, for man's inhumanity to man, the misfortunes of his people would sadden and exalt. It is true that he has assured William Archer[48] that his practical philosophy is meliorist; that his books are a plea against inhumanity to men, women and animals; that men make life worse than it need be; that they can get rid of a thousand ills; and that only by so doing, and by weighing results, may they know if good or evil predominates. But his writings do not make these purposes clear. And in the same breath with his meliorism, he quotes to Mr. Archer Sophocles' "not to have been born is best."

Classical, realistic and naturalistic as Hardy is in style, and architectonic in form, he is romantic in content and philosophy. "He does not become the life he deals with," says Mr. Abercrombie,[49] "but compels it all to become himself to fit in with a constant manner of intellectual judg-

[48] "Real Conversations. I, with Mr. Hardy" ("Critic," vol. 38).
[49] "Thomas Hardy, A Critical Study."

ment." The stars draw him out of himself now and then and the mood recorded in his *On a Fine Morning* gives him a glimpse of a brighter and healthier mental state; but Wessex and his broodings put him back in his prison of gloom again, whence issue his cries and lamentations.

Hence the classical Sophocles, for instance, is not his chief Greek affinity, but the romantic Aeschylus. In tragic moments, Aeschylean grandeur and revolt overturn Sophoclean grace and submission in him. *The Return of the Native* and *Jude the Obscure* are a far cry from "the *Daphnis and Chloe* lyricism" of *Under the Greenwood Tree;* from the Shellyan Platonism of *The Well-Beloved;* from the stoic resignation of Elizabeth-Jane in *The Mayor of Casterbridge*. Meantime, as we have seen, his poetry has grown steadily in disillusion and despair. Having finally read an anthropomorphic God out of the Universe, for all the good he is to man, he has lately buried him— reverently and regretfully, he admits—in *God's Funeral*. Yet surely the world is not sick to death over Fatalism. Disraeli shaped Destiny, and parodied Determinism in *The Infernal Marriage*. Mr. Wells in our own day admits the determinist's position, but adds, "I hestitate, I choose, just as though the thing were unknowable." He at least finds life endlessly interesting and profitable. Hardy is a greater artist, but his philosophy is not sufficiently thought out; he does not escape Fate mystically into a spirit world, nor practically by throwing himself with unremitting zeal into this: the whole spectacle saddens him and disheartens him. Say what his admirers will, he has suffered from limitation of education, on the one hand, and from a sensitive withdrawal, on the other, from affairs and from the society of his peers.

But we are not called upon to conclude pessimistically of the great pessimist. Many novel readers do not realize that Hardy has a philosophy, and others "skip" it. And though his world is not inspiriting, it is "full of beauty, sympathy, delicate perception, tenderness and tolerance."[50] And he leaves one of the great productions of our time,— *The Dynasts.*

The Dynasts is shapeless, confuses the arts[51] and preaches determinism throughout; but it transcends its philosophy and will endure as a work of genius. Its one hundred and thirty scenes present a panoramic view of the Napoleonic wars; its confusion of epic and drama does not disturb the reader and its Fatalism coincides with Justice in the fall of Napoleon. Spirits hover over the whole — not Meredithian spirits of comedy, but spirits of Irony and Pity — and convey the philosophy of the piece dramatically, like a Greek chorus. In his Preface Hardy declines to draw on mythology for gods "as sources or channels of Causation," thinking them out of place in the twentieth century because of "the wide prevalence of the monistic theory of the Universe."

One wishes Hardy would turn away from his later poetry and begin an epic-drama of the present conflict. He has said in conversation and in verse that war is doomed. Why should he not take his part in destroying it? A great work of art like *The Dynasts*, exposing the sins of nations, not the Unconsciousness of the Will, would close his work in glory.

---

[50] Jacob Salviris: "Westminster Review," vol. 178, p. 405.
[51] See Prof. Irving Babbit: "The New Laokoon," p. 232.